D1418495

# A SYSTEM FOR
# INSTRUCTION

# A SYSTEM FOR INSTRUCTION

**JOHN E. SEARLES**
The Pennsylvania State University

**INTERNATIONAL TEXTBOOK COMPANY**
Scranton, Pennsylvania

To David, Carolyn, Sarah, and Gordon

*it is to be hoped that you may understand*
*that the meaning of life is to laugh, to live . . .*
*but, also, it is to matter, to mean something . . .*
*to have it make some difference that you lived at all.*

# Preface

*My method is to take the utmost trouble to find the right thing to say, and then to say it with the utmost levity.*
　　　　　　　　　　　　　　　—George Bernard Shaw.

Teaching in modern schools is a weird and fascinating process. It is a whole composed of diverse parts; any penetration by analysis shows it to be a rather untidy process not readily susceptible to precise description. Much of it is art, some of it is science; many approaches are based on analysis, some on intuition, and, let's face it, a few on blind hope.

To write about teaching means to be forced into the same patterns, slightly untidy but fascinating. So this volume reflects in odd measure insights from observation, analysis from experimenters, distillations from wise minds, and speculations from active minds.

This diversity in teaching accounts for a diversity in tone and approach. In this book, a chapter is journalistic because much needs reporting; a chapter is encyclopedic because definitions must be established; a chapter is philosophic because a sense of order and logic is needed; a chapter is sociological-psychological because an objective analysis of the human must be attempted; a chapter is avuncular because advice is necessary; a chapter (or several) is technical because technique reflecting artistry and thought is necessary.

Teaching is a genuinely bemusing enterprise, taken all in all. The teacher is surrounded by the human condition with its tragedy, its comedy, its grandeur, and its ludicrousness. This, in turn, makes its mark on the tone of the book. If a serious subject is treated with levity, it is to avoid pedantry; if it is breezy, it is to blow away some of the dust of confusion; if it is aphoristic, it is from trying to be wise; if sentimental, it is to avoid emotionalism. The Biblical injunction is with us: "Let your speech be alway with grace, seasoned with salt."

To find the system and the order in the process and to show the wonder

and the glory in the effort; to challenge the mind and to quicken the spirit—
these are the aims. For it is as has been said by Gibran in *The Prophet*:

> If the teacher is indeed wise he does not bid you enter the house of
> his wisdom, but rather leads you to the threshold of your own mind.

I should like to express my gratitude to the host of people: the honest
critics and the false friends, the warm hearts and the wise minds, the serene
and the innocent, who, with human mixtures of concern and scorn, led me,
kicking and screaming, to the threshold of my own mind.

JOHN E. SEARLES

University Park, Pennsylvania
May, 1967

# Acknowledgments

Everyone is an expert on teaching, everyone is interested in teaching; everyone has been taught, everyone is a teacher. So the sources for this volume are many and varied. No claim is made that all have been covered. For permission to reprint material the author is grateful to the following:

The American Council on Education for quotations from "The Centrality of Education" by Adlai Stevenson in *The Educational Record*; Association for Supervision and Curriculum Development for selections from *Discipline* by George Sheviakov and Fritz Redl; David McKay Company, Inc., for selections from *The Taxonomy of Educational Objectives, Parts I and II*, by Benjamin Bloom and David Krathwohl; Harper and Row, Publishers, Inc., for selections from *Symbols, Signals, and Noise* by J. E. Pierce; *Harper's* Magazine, Inc., for "The Cultural Chasm" by Ralph Segalman; Harvard University Press for selections from *The Process of Education, On Knowing*, and *Towards a Theory of Education* by Jerome Bruner; Holt, Rinehart & Winston, Inc., for selections from *Teaching the New Social Studies* by Edwin K. Fenton; John Wiley & Sons, Inc., for material from *The Curriculum and the Disciplines of Knowledge* by Arthur King and John A. Brownell; McGraw-Hill Book Company for selections from *Realms of Meaning* by Philip Phenix; National Society for the Study of Education for selections from "Theories of Learning" by N. L. Gage in the 63rd Yearbook of the society, *Learning and Instruction*; *The New Yorker* for quotations from "Patriotic Tour and Postulate of Joy" by Robert Penn Warren; Random House, Inc., for quotations from *Coming of Age in America* by Edgar Z. Friedenberg; and *Saturday Review* for "Filling in the Spaces" by Melvin Lackey and selections from "Four Faces of Able Adolescents" by Elizabeth Drews.

J. E. S.

# Contents

## VARIATIONS ON THE THEME

## POSTLUDE

# PRELUDE

# chapter ONE

# An Introductory Passage

*There are more things in heaven and earth, Horatio, than are dreamt of in your philosophy.*—SHAKESPEARE.

Within the broad field called education lies a practice called instruction. This practice can be studied and described and, hence, added to the philosophic base from which the teacher proceeds in tackling the day-by-day tasks of instruction. The book probably will not bring heaven on earth for the instructor but it may extend his dreams for himself and his students.

This volume is written for those who will be practicing instruction in the new world of the 1970s and beyond. This world will be frightening because of one paramount and pervading idea: change. Knowledge, technologies, whole societies are changing in such degree and with such speed that about the only word that can be used is explosion—"population explosion," "knowledge explosion," "megalopolic explosion." These are big words for big ideas.

The drumming that heralds the coming of this new age is rather erratic and it is difficult to find the beat to which to march. However, there seems to be one rather steady beat; our society is moving into a period when education will be the major enterprise of that society, major to the degree that there will be a greater expenditure on education than on defense, and more employees will be in universities than in the Federal government. An estimate was made, in 1960, that education is a full-time occupation for nearly one-third of all Americans between age five and retirement.[1]

Consider these forces already in motion: The explosion in technology has taken us to the edges of the cybernetic revolution where machines have not only replaced human physical energy but are also replacing human mental energy. The next step is to raise the quality of human mental energy by probing the limits of mental abilities. The tool: education.

The explosion in technology has started a process of deification and

[1] Paul Woodring, "The Magnitude of the American Educational Establishment," *Saturday Review* (September 17, 1960), p. 71.

reification of the intellectual. How does a person in our mobile society move into this new elite? Education.

The population explosion adds more participants to the educational enterprise. One prediction serves: the University of California (one of three systems of public higher education in the most populous state) adds over 7,000 students per year and will have 273,000 by the year 2000.

As we find society changing, so do we find the educational enterprise changing. In the past few years much attention has been given to the whole enterprise, and there has been much soul searching about the field, as social enterprise, as actual process, and as a field of study. In this last context attention has been given of late to the central process of instruction. This focus is brought by an examination of the total pattern of the education process. Much thought has been given to what should be taught, much to how people learn, and there has been much description and analysis of the historical and social roots of our schools. Until the last few years, however, little of an analytic nature has been done on the instructional process. Now this area of study is catching up to the others, in quality if not in quantity.

The other areas of knowledge about schools and schooling have entered into the knowledge pattern given to those preparing to teach. It is time that knowledge of the instructional system takes its place in teacher preparation.

It is the purpose of this volume to synthesize and analyze some of the examinations of instruction and bring an ordered body of thought to the teacher who will engage in, or is engaged in, this instructional process.

The system described has the three parts of instructor, learner, and subject. These are all explored showing some of the nature of each and how each affects the decisions that a teacher has to make. The exploration of the learner and instructor are based on observation and reports of others; the idea of the subject is explored and graphically represented by means of a chart for criteria of search image choice that is developed throughout the volume.

The structure of this volume follows a cyclic pattern. The first cycle establishes the theme—the system of instruction—by defining that system within the broader social enterprise of instruction.

The second cycle develops this theme and penetrates further into the three parts of the system—the instructing of a subject, the instruction of students, and the instructor himself.

The third cycle describes variations on the theme that can be controlled by the instructor; that is, ways the system can be changed.

The instructor soon finds that the system is a rather melodious proposition. A sense of joy abounds as instructor and student play upon a thought in the same way musicians play upon a melody, a joy of discovery as the melody line is revealed in its thematic structure; a joy of fascination as the thought is embroidered by numberless variations on the theme; a joy of satisfaction as the completed thought hangs shimmering in the mind as a melody lingers on, at once both pleasing and tantalizing.

It is the quiet dream that this work may bring a sense of the glory and the challenge of instructing, a sense of its pattern and rhythm so that more may learn better and, more importantly, so that more may learn the joy of learning.

# THE THEME

# chapter TWO

# The Social Enterprise of Education

*If the Architect of the universe sends you a son, tremble. You cannot know if his soul will be good or evil. All you can do is be a loving father, protecting him until he reaches the age of twelve. From twelve until he is twenty, be his teacher. And from twenty on, be his friend.*—DON GUADALUPE.

In his definition of love, Don Guadalupe,[1] a wise but illiterate old man in his 70s, described with tender dignity his love of his children and pretty much summed up what education meant in a simpler time—when there was just the family, when there was a very small village, just a very small group of people who had the task of passing on their culture to their children.

But now we live in a different time and in a different way. Instead of a time of calm tranquility with little change, we live in a time of wild pandemonium and rapid change.

Don Guadalupe's injunction can shine before us as it has as long as man has searched for his humanity in himself and his family. But the world of our creation is so much with us that man's ever-renewing struggle toward humanity seems impeded by more and more of society.

Many forces mitigate against the friendship between a man and his son, the old and the young, this friendship that is needed so that education can take place.

These forces can well be examined in the context of the future; we may be too close to them now to see them clearly so let us look to a bench mark year, the year 2000, when these forces will have become clear.

Although it sounds rather far away, it comes closer when we remember that the children now in school will be spending over half their lives in the 21st century. If a function of education is to prepare a student for society,

---

[1] Michael Maccoby, "Love and Authority: A Study of Mexican Villagers," *Harpers Magazine* (March, 1964), p. 124.

the schools must prepare him for a society he will be living in, not for a bygone one. That will be the society of the 21st century.

## THE WORLD OF THE TWENTY-FIRST CENTURY

The year 2000 will see a continuation of the deep and wrenching changes that are in every sphere of our lives. These changes have a dimension of depth and also a dimension of speed that add immeasurably to the power of the change. In 1962 John F. Kennedy described the world of change in this way:

> Despite the striking fact that most of the scientists that the world has ever known are alive and working today, despite the fact that this nation's own scientific manpower is doubling every twelve years at a rate of growth more than three times that of our population as a whole, despite that—the vast stretches of the unknown and the unanswered and the unfinished still far outstrip our collective comprehension. No man can fully grasp how far and how fast we have come. But condense, if you will, the fifty-thousand years of man's recorded history into a time span of but half-century. Stated in these terms, we know very little about the first forty years, except that at the end of them advanced man had learned to use the skins of animals to cover himself. Then about ten years ago, under this standard, man emerged from his caves to construct other kinds of shelter. Only five years ago, man learned to write and use a cart with wheels. Christianity began less than two years ago. The printing press came this year and then, less than two months ago, during this whole fifty year span of human history, the steam engine provided a new source of power. Last month electric lights and telephone and airplanes became available. Only last week did we develop penicillin and television and nuclear power. And now, if America's new spacecraft succeeds in reaching the stars, we will literally have reached the stars before midnight tonight. This is a breathtaking pace, and such a pace cannot but help to create new ills as it dispels the old.[2]

**Social Changes in the Year 2000.** The overwhelming problem of the current age is the change in the social realm: the growth of the population. If ever there was a sword of Damocles hanging over civilization, it is the population explosion in the world today. This can be measured in many ways and described in many ways.

At the current rate of population growth in the world, in 450 years the population will be such that there will be one square meter of land per person.

Another way to look at population growth is to examine the rate of the doubling of population (see Fig. 2–1). It took something like 200 years for the population to double from 1650 to 1840. It doubled again from 1840 to 1930 (90 years). Then the rate for doubling was reduced to

[2] Speech at Rice University, Houston, Texas, on September 12, 1962.

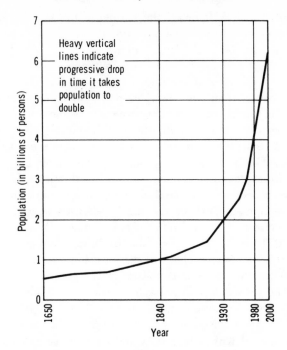

Fig. 2-1. Population curve; trends and rates.

50 years. It will take about 25 years to double again after 1980. In the year 2000 the rate of population doubling is going to be about every 15 or 20 years under this current growth.

What do these worldwide figures mean to our particular culture? We don't have to look at the year 2000 to get a sense of growth: 1965 to 1975 will suffice. This period reflects several population forces. One is the growth in numbers of people. Fewer people are dying, more people are being born— the rate of population growth is not changing too much, but the numbers are growing. We are also in the midst of a population shift from a rural culture to an urban culture. By this magic year of 2000, close to 90% of the people will be living in urban areas.

These two forces mean that in the period 1965 to 1970, the United States society is creating one million new households every year. It does not mean that we are creating new houses for people that are moving; it means creation of new households, new structures for new families.

What this means is the creation of a city the size of Chicago every year in the midst of a shift to urban areas which are already old and tired. This means the growth of a social problem of a magnitude that we have never tackled before. It means the crowding of millions of new people and new households into or around urban centers that are already overburdened, out of date, and obsolete. It makes the settling of the West look like something very simple and very straightforward.

**Changes in the Technological Realm.** There are some changes of vast magnitude in the technological realm which are summed up by the fact that we are in a period of a great revolution of power. We have moved, in a very few years, from the source of power in man's muscles through the harnessing of animal power to the harnessing of physical power through electricity. Now we are on the threshold of harnessing the power of the universe in the atom. Furthermore, all of this has happened within a short period of time. This physical energy that we have at our fingertips is also revolutionary in its amount. We have only to live through a blackout to see how much we depend on the physical energy of outside sources.

We are reaching a peak of the use of electrical energy and we are beginning to move now toward other energy sources. Who knows? Maybe by the year 2000 we will have been able to directly harness the energy of the sun to the point where people will not have to power a car by releasing the energy of the sun stored in petroleum in the ground and distilled into gasoline. Maybe we will get into a vehicle powered by silicon cells taking power directly from the sun and transmitting it directly to the wheels, without intermediary process. Maybe by then wheels will be out of date. Maybe we will walk around with a bare back and on that bare back will be one big silicon cell which will transmit energy right into us, and away we go. This is the revolution in physical energy, but is that all?

Right now in 1965–1966 we are on the threshold of the age of the harnessing of mental energy and we are creating highly complex machines capable of rudimentary mental work. We are calling them computers. In a few years some people may be calling them God, but right now we are calling them computers. The growth of the computers in numbers and ability to function is phenomenal. Their ability to memorize and their ability to weigh factors is such that they are now capable of making basic human decisions.

Now we are reaching a stage where the machinery created by men is making the decisions for men, the age of cybernetics. Where does this lead us? We are reaching a period where the harnessing of physical energy and mental energy will enable about 2% of our population to produce all the goods that are necessary for the other 98% of the people. This is production at our present level of affluence. This has startling social and value ramifications. The culture that we have had has always said that we must contribute by producing. Now we find that perhaps we can contribute by consuming.

Another technological change lies in the realm of biology. The biochemists are getting right at the heart of things. Through the unlocking of the DNA molecule they are beginning to understand the genetic arrangement of the human body. We are beginning to understand the chemical composition of the human body to a degree that we never thought of before.

We are having changes also in communication patterns. It is difficult to realize that television is a brand new thing. But there are still many people on the earth who experience amazement and wonder at watching by television as astronauts hurtle down out of the blue and land next to a carrier on which a television mechanism sends a signal back up to the heavens again and bounces it off a satellite and back down to the earth where it is transmitted and received instantaneously.

This revolution in communications is proceeding at an amazing pace. By 1975, according to authorities who are not science-fiction writers, anybody in the world will be able to talk to anybody else in the world with the proper use of communication satellites, sending his voice, his face, and documents. Nobody will be able to hide from anybody else. Another feature of communications is beginning to be explored—the use of laser beams. Theoretically, we can introduce enough information into one laser beam so that one laser beam will enable any person in the United States to communicate with any other person in pairs. One laser beam, if people could be arranged appropriately, would carry enough information so that the United States could pair off and each speak to his partner. No conversation would interrupt any other conversation, and the conversations could be held simultaneously. The whole pattern that is now on the skyline of urban America of miles of copper lines intersecting, each carrying messages, may be an anachronism.

The impact of technological change on our present society is dramatically illustrated by the effect of the automobile. In just one part of man's relation with his world, the struggle to be safe and secure, the impact has been tremendous.

> Out of every two cars now on the road, one will eventually be involved in an injury-producing accident; out of every two Americans, at the present rate, one will eventually be killed or hurt by an automobile. The increase in deaths caused by the automobile was only 3 per cent between 1951 and 1961, but in the years since 1961 they have increased by 25%.[3]

**Changes in the Political Realm.** In politics, as well, the speed and depth of change is being felt. One of the major changes is in the weaponry that man uses to assert his power. Man has not only created the power of energy for good, but also energy for destruction. We have now available to mankind power for destruction of an unbelievable magnitude. The only word that reflects the power is "overkill." Statistics from a book called *Our Depleted Society* graphically picture this concept: "If we had exploded an

[3] Eric Larrabee, "Written in Cold Fury," *Harper's Magazine* (April 1966), p. 117.

Hiroshima-sized bomb every day of the year for the past 1,965 years, the combined force would equal 14,000 megatons or about 70% of the present destructive capacity of present U.S. long-range bombers and missiles."[4]

There are other political changes of overwhelming importance in the international sphere. One is the rise of new states and the relationships between those states in a time when the power that we have is too powerful to use. In other words, we are in a position now where we have to find some other means of asserting international power. We must find in William James' phrase, "the moral equivalent of war." In the middle of this, new states are being formed. In 20 years we have doubled the number of states, all of which will have relationships with other states, carving out their own power patterns, their power areas, trying to find some means of assertion of that power short of destructive warfare. This is the pattern of international political change.

Another revolutionary change about these new states is in the phraseology of Adlai Stevenson, the "revolution of rising expectations." No longer are these states content to be what they were, but they are looking toward being something else. Right there lies another change in human society, which no longer is a series of separate societies: changes are bringing these societies closer together.

## EDUCATION IN THE YEAR 2000

We have spoken of some of the changes in this world of 2000. What about education in that particular world? Again the word "change" enters.

**The Effect of Social Changes in Education.** There is a change that makes education take a central place in the world of 2000. This change is the knowledge explosion. Ralph W. Tyler, who is one of the more influential social scientists in the country, made this statement: "Knowledge is being acquired at an exponential rate. This increases greatly the educational task of the secondary school. Today the high school graduate is expected to be as well educated as was a college graduate of fifty years ago."[5]

Society of the 21st century (if not that of today) will not be able to exist without a well-educated citizenry. For society to maintain the levels that seem to be indicated, a constant refreshment of knowledge and purpose is needed. This change is of such a degree that we can no longer trust the random patterns of education that we have had in society in the past years. More formal and patterned systems have to be used because the need for education is going to be so much greater. Not only is education going to be

---

[4] Seymour Melman, *Our Depleted Society* (New York: Holt, Rinehart and Winston, 1965), p. 14.

[5] Ralph W. Tyler, "The Knowledge Explosion and Its Implications," *Educational Record* (January, 1965), p. 152.

more ordered, but also it has to be more constant. In the past, society had to formally educate a person but once. When a citizen was young, he learned to speak, write, read, and maybe he learned a little about the culture around him. Then he went off to work in that culture and that's all there was to it until he died, generally at around forty years of age. Now this life period is extended and has so many more changes in it that people will have to be reeducated as they go along.

One study of college education in the year 2000 predicted that everybody will have to have a formal education three times in his life. The first period will have the same purpose as now, to prepare the citizen for some period of contribution in that life. Then, because his job will change at least three times in his work period, he will have to be reeducated in some way or another. Then, because he will retire at a predicted retirement age of 55, he will have to be reeducated for the retirement years.

Life will form itself into three distinct periods for a person. The first one, the period of being withheld from society—we call it adolescence now—until he is about 25; then a period of productivity until he is about 55; then a period of retirement from 55 on. By 2000 the life expectancy will certainly be 85 years of age, if not more. So life will be divided into thirds; only one-third of his life will be what we have called an adult contribution to society.

What will this mean for education? It will mean vast proliferation of the educational system to take care of all the demands. By the year 2000 the central social enterprise is going to be the enterprise of education.

A very interesting phenomenon happens. The speech by President Kennedy referred to above included the sentence, "The greater our knowledge increases, the greater our ignorance unfolds." The more knowledge we accumulate, the more we are driven to understand what we have accumulated and to accumulate more. This gives an accelerating force to the centrality of education.

Another effect on education occurs at the actual operative level when all this technology is married with the necessity for education. It might be well to pause here and explore this idea by examining the classroom of 1999 where the student will be bringing an apple to the computer.

**The Classroom of the Year 2000.** "History," said H. G. Wells in the beginnings of this century, "is more and more a race between education and catastrophe." This race has become more gruesome in the middle of this century with the entry of technology overwhelmingly on the side of catastrophe.

But technology is also being used, haltingly and reluctantly, on the side of education and perhaps by the end of the century new technologies will allow education to draw closer to its opponent in this race.

By 1999, the classroom as we now know it will have changed. Today's large room with thirty to forty desks facing a larger one will be supplemented by an "inquiry station," a comfortable private area complete with a small console lined with buttons and a typewriter. The inquiry station, as a self-contained unit, can be located anywhere: school, home, office building, unused basement.

The teacher gains new dignity, as witness the replacement of his present paperstrewn, overloaded headquarters by a private office, a consulting room like that of a physician or lawyer or psychiatrist. Its dominant feature, like that of the inquiry station, is a machine, but a more complicated one, capable of receiving and instantly transcribing messages, much as a teletype does now. More important than the visual effect is the change in the educational process. How does little Willie, class of '99, tackle a new subject? Let us watch him.

First he meets the teacher. Through a personal interview, the teacher can ascertain, as he does now, Willie's background, drives, and abilities in the subject to be taught and assigns certain "programs" to be mastered. Willie then goes to the proper inquiry station where he notifies the machine by flipping a switch or dialing that he is present and eager to begin. The machine responds, greeting him by name and quickly typing out initial directions. This may be to ask Willie to read a few pages in an accompanying text and then answer a few questions.

It is a time-honored technique among teachers which recognizes the book for what it is, a superb teaching tool. It is also time consuming for a teacher and *each* student; hence, the machine.

Then Willie turns back to the machine, which has been measuring the time interval to check on his reading and learning speed. The machine types a question, receives an answer, judges it, and gives an immediate evaluation. Then it gives another question, based on the response to the previous question. Thus proceeds the lesson.

When Willie has mastered this material to the satisfaction of himself and the machine, he returns to the teacher. The teacher has had the results, and also a running commentary of Willie's performance typed out for him on his copy by the machine.

Teacher and pupil can now sit down to *real* teaching-learning. All the preliminaries of gaining background knowledge, vocabulary, and skills have been achieved, and Willie comes prepared to the teacher. They can sit down to the intensely human situation of pondering the imponderables, creating new ideas and evaluating old constructs and perceptions. Wisdom and youth have their ancient, honorable and fascinating confrontation.

Thus, the teacher assumes a more exalted position in the process of education as a result of technology. By using the computer both as a storehouse of information and a means of efficient dissemination, he has left himself free for the best kind of teaching.

Questions immediately arise. Among them are these: Aren't these too far in the future? Can the idea of programming fit all areas of knowledge and be susceptible to computer use? Will this replace the teacher? And most importantly, will it teach anything? Let's look at these questions.

All of the processes mentioned have already been developed. We must remember also that technology expands knowledge at an overwhelming rate. In this area the safest prediction is that any prediction is too conservative.

One reaction to these ideas is that they are all right for teaching *some* subjects; generally, sequential subjects that depend for mastery on memorization of steps. As of now, the research and experimentation have been done with such subjects as foreign languages, stenotypy, and elementary statistics. These subjects have the necessary orderliness. More research and experimentation are needed, of course, to ascertain if this necessary orderliness can be found in other areas. One area of promise may lie in the use of an organizational technique that might be called "problem simulations," which in a certain sense takes its cue from games theory.

Perhaps these simulations can be established around areas that require decision making and thus be susceptible to this orderliness.

Also, there is a characteristic of programming these machines that makes it seem possible that they can be used for many subjects: it is flexibility.

Will computer-assisted instruction replace the teacher? This is an obvious question but, nonetheless, a pressing one. We have tried to point out that the machine will supplement the teacher and enable a good teacher to be a better one. But there is another answer to the question. These machines had better not replace the teacher. The year 1984 comes before 1999, or putting it another way, machines are without a sense of values and will serve their masters, Orwellian or otherwise. Because of this, care must be taken that the machine serves the teacher and not the other way around. It might be easy for the teacher to give in, to accept predetermined programming, and to let it be the final end of his teaching. Confusion of means and ends here could be disastrous because of the potential involved.

Will the computer teach adequately? It is in this area that we determine if computer-based instruction is a definite aid or just a gimmick. There is much to support the former contention. Uttal, from his experiences in teaching with computers states: "Computer teaching is feasible. We have been delighted with the ease with which some of the rules of learning have been embodied and with the broad applicability of computer-based teaching machines to many different types of material."[6]

Among the "rules" of learning which are embodied in this type of

[6] W. R. Uttal, "On Conversational Interaction" in John E. Caulson, *Programmed Training and Computer Instruction,* Proceedings of the Conference on Application of Digital Computers to Automated Instruction (New York: John Wiley & Sons, Inc., 1962).

instruction are such ideas as feedback for immediate reinforcement and a high motivation on the part of the learner.

One of the best teaching mechanisms is the human tutor engaging in conversational interaction with the student. Uttal claims that "the computer allows us to approach full simulation of the human tutorial process."

Given these ideas of a sound psychological basis and simulation of a sound procedure, it seems logical to assume good teaching *can* take place using computer-based techniques.

We must put a rein to our fancy and return to the present and turn to an examination of our present educational system and establish some definitions.

## A VIEW OF EDUCATION AS SOCIAL ENTERPRISE

Education now, and in 2000, is a product ("he is educated"), a process ("I am being educated"), a study ("I am a professor of education"), as well as a social enterprise. The whole terminology gets a bit slippery and some patterns need to be defined a bit.

**Macroeducation and Microeducation.** Within the realm of education there are two patterns. One of them, macroeducation, has to do with educational policy planning, with the broader philosophic bases of education, sociological bases of education, the relationship of schools to other media for education, the fascinating studies of such things as: how much money should be alloted to education, how much does the society gain from having an educated populace, economic inputs of educated people versus noneducated people. Macroeducational studies deal with the reaction of educational systems and patterns to the political, social, and economic sectors of human endeavor.

More pertinent to us is the study of microeducation, which focuses on what happens in the classroom. This study divides itself into three areas: (a) the curriculum—what should be taught; (b) the learning process—how learning comes about; and (c) the process of instruction—how to structure knowledge in another mind.

This last becomes the central part of this book. We shall set about exploring and examining the system whereby, in the formal, ordered context of schooling, knowledge and ideas are structured and become part of the learner's mind and behavior.

One more task faces us before we leave this discussion of the social enterprise of education. What does education try to do in the social order? What is the purpose?

**The Purpose of Education.** It might sound quite simplified, but it seems that the main purpose of education has to do with constantly refreshing a society by a continual reexamination of society and knowledge. This examination is aimed at bringing the learner from innocence to wisdom on a path that steers between trauma and folly.

Adlai Stevenson, in a speech at the University of Illinois a few months previous to his death, described the problem and purpose of education in a world of change:

> . . . We shall not, in the coming decades, slow down very much the tempo of dynamic change. The external stimuli to fear and hence to unreason will not slacken. We must therefore try to modify people's reactions to them, and it is here, above all, I suggest, that the vital import of education must be seen. The politics of fear and unreason are, precisely, the politics of ignorance. This way lies destruction and ruin.
>
> We can get through the vast interlocking social revolutions of our day on one condition only—that we face them with the information and with the balance that educaetion alone can give.
>
> It is not simply a matter of the facts. It is also an attitude *to* the facts. It is readiness to look at problems from different angles. It is ability to enter imaginatively into the minds of others. It is a dogged determination to weigh evidence and to look reality in the face. It is the self-knowledge that distinguishes between principle and self-interest. It is the insight that is derived from past experience, weighed and digested. How right was Santayana when he said: "Men who will not learn from history are destined to repeat it." Above all, it is the wisdom that comes from a largeness of vision, a generosity of spirit which only contact with the greatest minds and treasures of civilization can bring.
>
> Indeed, the final end of all true education is precisely this wisdom which enhances learning, dignifies human relations, and plays, with a sort of benign tolerance, over the follies and shortcomings of all God's children.
>
> Therefore, as the fruit and crown of your education, I would wish you nothing more precious than this spirit of wisdom. Nor do I know any more moving words to describe it than those in which it is said of wisdom:
>
> "I am the mother of fair love and of fear and of knowledge and of holy hope. In me is all grace of the way and of the truth, in me all hope of life and virtue. . . ."[7]

So, in our passage from innocence to wisdom, let us now turn, with fair love, fear, and holy hope, to a look at knowledge.

## SUGGESTED READINGS

BRAMELD, THEODORE. *Education for the Emerging Age* (New York: Harper & Row, Publishers, 1961).

CONANT, JAMES B. *Slums and Suburbs* (New York: McGraw-Hill Company, 1961).

[7] Adlai Stevenson, "The Centrality of Education," *Educational Record* (Fall, 1965), p. 345.

CREMIN, LAWRENCE. *The Transformation of the School* (New York: Alfred A. Knopf, Inc., 1962).

GARDNER, JOHN. *Self Renewal: The Individual and the Innovative Society* (New York: Harper & Row, Publishers, 1964).

LIEBERMAN, MYRON. *The Future of Public Education* (Chicago: Phoenix Books, University of Chicago Press, 1962).

WEINER, NORBERT. *The Human Use of Human Beings* (New York: Houghton Mifflin Company, 1950).

# chapter THREE

# The Educational Enterprise of Instruction

*Education is the acquisition of the art of utilization of knowledge.*—ALFRED NORTH WHITEHEAD.

To give the balance and the information that will enable our society to get through the vast interlocking social revolutions of our day much of the public enterprise is now concerned with education. This public enterprise is large and attention must be paid to one part that will get more prominent—the microeducation, particularly the system of instruction. For it is in the schools, in the formal process of instructing, that the focus is on the acquisition of knowledge and of the art of utilization of knowledge.

Much research and thought have been given to this process of instruction and the resultant body of knowledge has begun to take on a structure to the degree that it can form the basis for a disciplined inquiry. In short, the system of instruction can be learned by people who wish to teach and can become arrows in the quiver as the teacher enters the lists in the battle to dispel ignorance.

## THE DISCIPLINE OF INSTRUCTION

If there is a disciplined body of knowledge that can be called instruction, it has certain limits and a certain context. The context we discussed in the previous chapter. The delimitations we can best describe by developing some contrasts with other factors in education that are similar but not precisely the same.

**The Art of Teaching and the Science of Instructing.** At first blush, this distinction might seem to be an artificial one of the type that characterizes much of the writing about education and gives the reader the sinking "here-we-go-again" feeling. But again we must look to the future world in which you will live. As remarked before, this transitory pulsation between birth and death that we call life is going to be lived under the impact of a great deal of information coming from all directions. This random information is all going to be organized to communicate something to someone. But also, in this coming age, there will also have to be an ordering of vast amounts of information. This is the point of difference between teaching and instruction. Teaching is any imparting of information that leads to learning; instruction is the imparting of *ordered* information. There is a pattern and a structure to the information. Look to the root of the word: instruction means to place in a structure. In this instance a structure of an idea, or of a conditioning, or a psychomotor skill.

This distinction might seem rather precious at this time but in another few years, as random information increases its impact on individuals, the distinction will have to be made. Even today the distinction is made: the dictionaries make it in the same way. Now it has to penetrate into the schools, the social organization designed for instruction.

**The Act of Learning and the Act of Instructing.** Another basic distinction that needs to be made in order to set up a definition of instruction is the difference between learning and instruction. Gage, in one of the basic books that deals with the growing discipline of instruction,[1] says:

> While theories of learning deal with the ways in which an organism learns, theories of teaching deal with the ways in which a person influences an organism to learn.
>
> To rephrase the thesis: Although theories of learning are necessary to the understanding, prediction and control of the learning process, they cannot suffice in education. The goal of education—to engender learning in the most desirable and efficient ways possible—would seem to require an additional science and technology of teaching. To satisfy the practical demands of education, theories of learning must be "stood on their head" so as to yield theories of teaching.

What is happening is the growth of a new field, rather narrow but quite important, under the broad umbrella of education, the field of instruction. While its purpose is to bring about learning, it focuses on the processes by which an organism can be influenced to learn. Where learning theory looks upon learning as a process (as it must) instruction theory looks upon learning as a product.

The development of instruction theory seems to be particularly necessary in the field of teacher preparation. After studying learning theory, the question remains in the teacher's mind, "How shall I teach?" Gage maintains,

[1] N. L. Gage, "Theories of Teaching," in *Theories of Learning and Instruction,* Ernest Hilgard, ed., Sixty-Third Yearbook of National Society for Study of Education (Chicago: University of Chicago Press, 1964), pp. 168–169.

. . . teachers must know how to manipulate the independent variables, especially their own behaviors, that determine learning. Such knowledge cannot be derived automatically from knowledge about the learning process. *To explain and control the teaching act requires a science and a technology in its own right.*" [Italics added.][2]

So it is now incumbent on us to develop the theories and isolate the principles that will become the science and technology of instruction.

This, of course, does not deny the importance of the learning process in such a scheme. What it does do is put it in its proper place by saying in effect that learning is the goal and product of instruction but that instruction is an ordered process that can enhance learning. Learning focuses on the student, instruction focuses on the teacher. Past experience seems to show that knowledge of theories of learning alone cannot totally improve classroom performance. So we must turn to a study of the instruction process.

**The Pattern of Communication and the Pattern of Instruction.**   As instruction differs from learning, it also differs from communication. The difference is not the same, however. In a real sense, instruction is a process within the broader pattern of communication. This distinction must be made in the modern world, which is feeling the impact of communications theory. Man, in his constant restless search for meaning, has begun to define and clarify the vast arena of communication, and the words "communication revolution," "information theory," "communications theory" have attained a glamour because they conjure up images of the new breed as it works with its banks of computers to do battle with the world's ills, real and fancied. Out of this has come a new vocabulary that has a seductive fascination. So before we succumb perhaps it is best to examine these theories and test their application to instruction. A representative definition of the term communication is: "Broadly: The establishment of a social unit from individuals, by the use of language or signs. The sharing of common sets of rules, for various goal-seeking activities."[3]

This gives an idea of the breadth of the area within which communications theorists work. To say that instruction is the same as communication is to say that electing a President is the same as politics.

Interestingly enough the communications theorists themselves do not set themselves as Pied Pipers poised to free us from all rats. Pierce in a study of communications points out that "communications theory has its origins in the study of electrical communication,"[4] and goes on to discuss its applicability to other fields. He ends his discussion of the relation of

---

[2] *Ibid.*, p. 273.

[3] Colin Cherry, *On Human Communication* (New York: John Wiley & Sons, Inc., 1961), p. 303. Also see pp. 3–8.

[4] J. E. Pierce, *Symbols, Signals and Noise: The Nature and Process of Communication* (New York: Harper & Row, Publishers, 1961), p. 24.

information theory (he uses communication and information theory inter-changeably) and psychology with the thought:

> . . . I myself think that information theory has provided psycholo-gists with a new and important picture of the process of communication and with a new and important measure of the complexity of a task. It has also been important in stirring psychologists up, in making them re-evaluate old data and seek new data. It seems to me, however, that while information theory provides a central universal structure and organization for electrical communication, it constitutes only an attractive area in psychology. It also adds a few new and sparkling expressions to the vocabulary of workers in other areas.[5]

So let these words be a wise warning to us. Communications theory can be an analog for the instruction process; it can add a few new, sparkling expressions as we attempt a description and analysis of the instruction process. It is analagous to, but not synonomous with, instruction.

**The Constriction of Indoctrination and the Constraint of Instruction.** One final difference must be made as a prelude to a definition of instruction. Educators suffer quite a crisis of conscience as they struggle with the weighty moral problem of the position of indoctrination in the educational system for a free society. In this volume we shall look upon instruction as a process dependent upon the inquiring mind of the participants: instructor and pupil. Indoctrination is outside of this definition in that it seems to be a more emotional act dependent upon an unchallenging acceptance by the participants of ideas to be inculcated.

## A SYSTEM OF INSTRUCTION

Instruction is a process for the implanting of a structure in a mind. This in-structuring results from a search for meaning in the structure. This search forms a coherent ternary system which has as components the idea, the "mind" of the instructor, and the "mind" of the learner. The process in the system seems to be something like this: In the dialog that constitutes this search, the instructor has a search image of the structure of the idea under consideration, and he shapes his teaching decisions by measuring the feed-back from the learning mind to the search image he holds.

This proposition introduces a "new and sparkling vocabulary" and it is this that must be examined now. It is the thesis of this work that the process of instruction can be defined and that certain principles can be derived and that therefore instruction can be called a science. Most im-portantly, others can be let in on the secret. So let us look upon this as an instruction about instruction and begin to define this new vocabulary.

[5] *Ibid.*, p. 249.

SYSTEM: a set or arrangement of things so related or connected as to form a unity or organic whole; a regular, orderly way of doing something; order; method; regularity.

Thus does the dictionary define this concept. So when we define and declare instruction to be a system, we mean that its parts interrelate and interconnect so as to form a total entity that is more than a sum of its parts, which is a definition of *structure*. Within this system there are the three interrelated parts: the *search image*, the *instructor*, and the *learner*.

The LEARNER: the mind at which instruction is aimed. In Bruner's words, "Instruction is a provisional state that has as its object to make the learner or problem-solver self-sufficient."[6]

This rather apparent idea may make the reader plead for mercy but it is necessary to look at the implication of the idea that it is the aim of instruction to make the learner self-sufficient. The system is designed with two purposes: the in-structuring of the search image and the development of an ability to learn. This latter then means that there is a necessary ingredient of the system, a certain reaching out by the learner toward the search image. This process, when given direction, regularity, and order becomes what we will call *inquiry*.

The INSTRUCTOR: the person responsible for the system, and for guiding and shaping the process until something in the way of a learning of the search image has taken place.

Again, before we are accused of beating the reader over the head with the obvious, let us hasten to point out the implication in this definition. This means that the teacher is the decision maker; he has certain choices and alternatives for plans of action, and, because the system is orderly, he can make these decisions in an organized, rational way. Research has not progressed to the point that probability theory can predict the outcomes of the decisions before they are made but it may be able to do so before the century is over. It becomes apparent from this that the instructor is a central participant in the process of instruction and therefore, when this system is optimally operative, there will not be the student complaint, "Gee, do we gotta do what we wanta do today again?"

The SEARCH IMAGE: the immediate learning task in the system. Generally small, well-ordered, and learnable, it can be in the cognitive, affective, or psychomotor domain. We limit the discussion to the cognitive.

In order to round out this idea of the image to be searched for in the instruction system it is necessary to scratch around under the surface of the definition and examine its parts and derivations. In short let us try to order

[6] Jerome Bruner, "Theorems on Instruction," in Ernest Hilgard, *op. cit.*, pp. 318–319.

the concept of search image. Perhaps the best way to demonstrate this order is by way of a model, such as in Fig. 3–1.

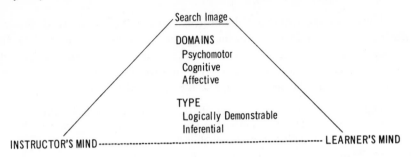

NOTE: This fits into a complete model for this system found in Chapter 4. Further elements of the parts of the system will be added in Chapters 5, 6, and 9.

FIG. 3-1. Elements of parts of the system.

The concept of search image has a structure of its own and we start with an examination of two of the parts of that structure: the domain of the search image and the type of search images.

*Domain* refers to the educational objectives[7] and becomes three broad categories of search images. That is to say that some of these search images are essentially psychomotor or manipulative skills, some are cognitive (which have to do with the understanding of knowledge and the growth of intellectual abilities and skills), and some are essentially affective (which deal with interests, attitudes, and values and the development of appreciations and adequate adjustment).

The *type* of search image refers to the means of verification of the knowledge. There are two: the logically demonstrable and the inferential.

*The logically demonstrable* is an idea or a reality that can be deemed true by a mental process that can sift through irrelevancies and test this assertion and label it true. Learners can be instructed rather quickly in this type of knowledge but, most importantly, they can and must be taught the pattern of sorting.

There is no either/or aspect to these two types of knowledge. As Conant says in his conclusions to his essay describing two modes of thought: "There should be places . . . for those who from early youth desire to study human problems by empirical methods and also places for those who are interested in broad speculative theories."[8] Knowledge is found in both areas, and the search by the student must not be limited to one; however, the instructor

[7] Benjamin S. Bloom, *Taxonomy of Educational Objectives* (New York: David McKay Company, Inc., 1956), p. 7. See also Chapters 5 and 6 of this volume.

[8] James B. Conant, *Two Modes of Thought* (New York: Pocket Books, Inc., 1964), p. 93.

must distinguish between these two broad areas so that the appropriate method of inquiry may be used by the student in the instructional system described before.

The inferential is a means of derivation of knowledge based on three logical processes: deduction, induction, and analogy. Much has been made over the distinction of inductive and deductive thought processes and which is proper for the best type of learning. Rather than make this either/or choice it might be well to remember Whitehead's point:

> There is a tradition of opposition between adherents of induction and deduction. In my view, it would be just as sensible for the two ends of a worm to quarrel. Both observation and deduction are necessary for any knowledge worth having.[9]

This type of search image, the inferential, is one that is reached by the learner after a logical thought process that determines the validity of the bit of knowledge. This introduces the idea that learning can have results of both product and process, an idea which is developed in Chapter 5. Chapter 8 contains a further exploration of deductive and inductive processes.

## POWER INPUTS INTO THE SYSTEM FOR INSTRUCTION

We have described a system that is essentially static but in order for the system to produce any results it must become a process. Wheels have to turn. And before wheels can turn there must be power. Where does the system obtain the power to make it a process? The latter paragraphs of the above section give some hints. It seems straightforward to assume that there are an intellectual and an emotional power component. Ideas become powerful when there is an attraction (emotional power) or a utility (intellectual power).

Examination of the role of power in the system of instruction shows that the input comes from two sources—the mind of the instructor and the mind of the learner.

**Power Inputs by the Instructor.** Search images can be given, as noted above, an intellectual and an emotional power. The intellectual power comes from the proper selection of the order of the search image, selected so as to be intellectually honest and relevant. This sounds rather moralistic but nothing is more powerful than an idea whose time has come.

But intellectual power is often an unattractive power and color has to be added to it by an emotional power (as if they could be separated, anyhow). The teacher can and must add a motivating power to the search image. It

---

[9] Alfred Whitehead, *The Aims of Education* (New York: The New American Library of World Literature, Inc., 1929), p. 119.

is in this part of the system of instruction that technology is being felt. The machinery of Madison Avenue can be used to great effect, and there is every reason to believe that the schools have barely begun to explore the potential of instructional media.

**Power Inputs by the Learner's Mind.** Learning no less than invention is 10 percent inspiration and 90 percent perspiration but, as in the case of many aphorisms, this is more dramatic than accurate. For complete accuracy we have to use far less colorful phrases for perspiration. We must be mundane and substitute the idea that much of the effort of the student must be *motivation*—the force that impels the reaching out for the search image. Or in the phrase used before, a power input for the system.

Motivation is but one of the classes of power inputs by the student mind. But motivation is the *sine qua non*; it gives a necessary predisposition to learning.

Here we have the first step in the system of instruction; the system will work only with this power input from the student mind. Often the first task of the instructor is to somehow overcome a mental lethargy and change potential energy to kinetic energy.

Secondly, an ability is needed to sort the relevant from the irrelevant. With this attitude the student mind can turn to certain activities that provide a power input for the system. These are powers of analysis based on examination of premises and evidence and on inferential reasoning. If this sounds like the description of the types of search image described above, it is designed to.

That is just the point. The function of the system of instruction is to provide a coherent structure which coincides with the structure of the search image, the act of instruction in the ordering of the knowledge, and the restructuring by the learner.

This necessary coincidence leads to the next point which is central to the whole concept of the system of instruction.

## THE RECIPROCAL RELATIONSHIP AMONG THE COMPONENTS

What naturally results from the power inputs of the instructor and the student is a *dialog*. This implies a movement back and forth across a channel of communication as instructor and student examine a search image. In the "new and sparkling expressions" this can be called input, throughput, and output. Without this dialog, instruction cannot take place; "telling" is the better verb for the attempt to instruct without a dialog.

This dialog facilitates learning. On any level it will make for more interesting classrooms. Not every dialog will be of intellectual penetration— most will not. But that is a relative term and, when the student is new to the search image that is the subject of the instruction, there probably will be little intellectual penetration on absolute terms but a great deal in the relative terms of the participating minds. To paraphrase the poet, "It's better to have dialoged and fallen short than never to have dialoged at all!"

The reciprocity in this dialog comes from the mutual interaction of the three components mentioned before.

This reciprocity in relationship among the three parts becomes the necessary ingredient of the system, the process of inquiry. This process is the searching for knowledge through ordered procedures; the instructor must provide an order for the knowledge and instruct the student in an orderly process for thinking.

## THE ORDERING OF KNOWLEDGE

We have introduced another concept that needs definition here and further elaboration in later chapters. In this context, the ordering of knowledge refers to the structure of an idea, its parts, and the way they are interrelated. It is more than that: it is the order in which these are brought to the attention of the learner. Order has two meanings: a pattern ("let me put my thoughts in order") and a sequential arrangement ("The Presidents in order of importance . . . or chronological order"). These two definitions are not firmly discrete and both have their position in the ordering of knowledge: the sequential arrangement of the structure in order (another meaning) to place that structure in a pattern that will facilitate learning. In this sense, ordering of knowledge in the system for instruction becomes the major teacher act in the cognitive domain.

There is another dimension to this ordering of knowledge. We have spoken of the ordering *within* a search image but must add to it the ordering of search images into larger patterns. Each bit of knowledge must be ordered within and related without to a larger order. The system of instruction leads the learner through an ordered sequence within an image and from one image to another.

Then what is the proper sequence? It is impossible to determine this in the abstract because it is dependent upon the knowledge to be taught and the state of the learner's mind at the given time. However, some rules for sequencing will be discussed in Chapter 8 when we discuss the ordering of knowledge.

A pattern begins to emerge here. If there is a definite sequence of procedure in what might be called the "infrastructure" and the "suprastructure," why hasn't it been captured and put into teaching? In a word, it has.

**Programmed Instruction.** Much experimentation has been done on the use of placing ordered knowledge in a specified sequence—programmed—for self-instruction. Programmed instruction has been called "a truly revolutionary device." It will not be revolutionary to the degree that it will threaten the system of instruction or replace the instructor in that system. ". . . It is revolutionary, not so much in itself, as in its ability to interact with certain other developments in education. . . . [It will be] one of an arsenal of teaching devices at the command of the teacher to help him to do his job better."[10] These are the words of one authority commissioned to examine the position of programmed instruction, today and tomorrow. What is this new weapon in the arsenal?

Schramm defines the elements of programmed instruction:

a) an ordered sequence of stimulus items
b) to each of which a student responds in some specified way,
c) his responses being reinforced by immediate knowledge of results,
d) so that he moves by small steps,
e) therefore making few errors and practicing mostly correct responses,
f) from what he knows, by a process of successively closer approximation, toward what he is supposed to learn from the program.

All of this sounds much like the system of instruction described in this chapter. And it is. A good instructor, with a carefully organized plan, does engage in programmed instruction and does it well. However, if we add another element to the programmed instruction, that of the "hardware" (some type of teaching machine), we see the new weapon. The machine adds two main advantages: (1) It can reach the learner individually so that he can work at his own speed and receive his own reinforcement and (2) it does not get tired and lose its temper. It can work constantly and in the same way. It is not only patient, it is implacable.

There are some demurrers entered about this. The major objections center around the impersonality of the process with its concomitant to force a sterile thought pattern and to inhibit creative flights. This sequence, given as an example, rather irreverently jibes at programmed instruction.[11]

## FILLING IN THE SPACES

HELLO THERE!
We want to show you a sample of your new lesson guide.
You will be using this new lesson guide and we think you will be happier
    if you know how it works.
So please go on to the next card.

VERY GOOD!
We asked you to go on to the next card, which is this one, and you did.
That's just fine.
You are doing very well.
Now please go on to the next card.

[10] Wilbur Schramm, *Programmed Instruction* (New York: Fund for the Advancement of Education, 1962), pp. 1, 4.

[11] Prepared by Melvin Lackey, U.S. Naval Dental School. Quoted in *Saturday Review* (August 17, 1963), p. 39.

FINE!
Here you are on the third card already.
Now we can start the game. Here is how we play it.
Each card has lots of words on it, telling you something.
But some of the words will be left out, and you will have to fill them in.
    Like on the next card.
Go on to it, please.

DANDY!
So when you see a space where a word should be, you fill it in. With
    your pencil.
When the word is left out, you will see a space ————.
Write the word in the ————.
And go on to the next card.

WHOOPS!
Did you write anything in the ————?
You were bad and did not follow instructions.
You must not think you are so smart.
You must do what we say and write the w———— in the space. And
    then go on to the next card where you will see the missing word
    at the top.
Like on the next card.

WORD
That is very good.
Did you write it tiny so that it fit the space?
All right. Now we will sum up what we have said and get on with the
    lesson guide.
Next card pl————.

PLEASE
On each card of the lesson guide, there will be a missing word.
Where the word is missing, there will be a space for you to fill in.
You will go from card to card, filling the spaces.
With words.
Perhaps you've caught on by now. You f———— in the spaces.

FILL
Perhaps, too, you are rather tired of filling in the spaces.
Perhaps you think you don't learn so much by f———— in the sp————.

FILLING IN THE SPACES
Perhaps you think there's something more to learning that just filling
    in the spaces.
If so, you are a real s———— o———— b————.

SHREWD OBSERVER, BUSTER
Because there is.

From this discussion, it can be discerned that the objections to the idea
are not with programming but with its implementation in the classroom. It
is this that leads to the conclusion that programming is a force that will be
used more and more. It is sound in theory; the next step is properly putting

it into practice, particularly the development of programs that will meet the objections and retain the advantages.

## SUGGESTED READINGS

BARZUN, JACQUES. *The House of Intellect* (New York: Harper & Row, Publishers, 1959).

HIGHET, GILBERT. *The Art of Teaching* (New York: Vintage Books, Random House, Inc., 1955).

LUMSDAINE, A. A. "Educational Technology, Programmed Learning and Instructional Science," in Ernest Hilgard, ed., *Theories of Learning and Instruction*, Sixty-Third Yearbook of National Society for the Study of Education (Chicago: The University of Chicago Press, 1964).

SCANDURA, JOSEPH. "Teaching—Technology or Theory," *Journal of Educational Research* (Spring, 1966), pp. 139–145.

# chapter FOUR

# A Model for the System

*They can have any model they wish as long as it is black.*—HENRY FORD (paraphrased).

We have outlined speculations about education as it will be, schools as they must be, and instruction as it is and could be. We have delved into the idea of instruction as a system, exploring its separate parts of the search image and subject, the learner mind in the system and the instructor's mind in the system.

One of the best ways to examine the functioning of a system is to establish a model of it. In the terminology established in the first part of this volume, this model becomes the search image for the instructor as the process unfolds. To paraphrase a seasonally fashionable rhyme:

'Twas the moment before learning and all through the minds,
Visions were stirring of all of the kinds,
The teacher was snuggled down deep in his work
With instruction models, the poor muddled jerk.

This piteous plaint is designed to dramatize the task of the instructor. He has the mental juggling act of chasing two search images: (1) the bit of knowledge that is central in the system of instruction and (2) the model of the system of instruction itself.

It is to this latter that we now address ourselves. A model is a handy mental device to portray a rather complex interrelationship of a system. The model suggested here is not the only one that could be utilized. Many others could be brought forward; it might not be too much to say that any perceptive person could make his own after a few years of experience.

This paradigm illustrates the system of instruction of that system and shows how four variations, generally independent of the system, act on it and have an effect on it.

This will not be a compendium of helpful hints for happy teaching; rather it will be a description and analysis of the arenas within which the

33

instructor will make his own decisions. The model can show what decisions must be made; the actual choice must await the particular situation.

## THE PARTS OF THE MODEL

Let us turn now to the model in its totality and then describe its various parts. Figure 4-1 shows the model.

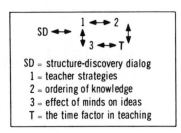

SD = structure-discovery dialog
1 = teacher strategies
2 = ordering of knowledge
3 = effect of minds on ideas
T = the time factor in teaching

Fig. 4-1.

**The Structure-Discovery Dialog.** This dialog (SD) is the process of instruction. It contains the three components of (1) the search image for the bit of knowledge, (2) the instructor's mind, and (3) the learner's mind. To put the system into motion there are power inputs from the instructor as he imparts the structure to the search image. Perhaps the best way to define it is through the medium of a model for this dialog, which is shown in Fig. 4-2.

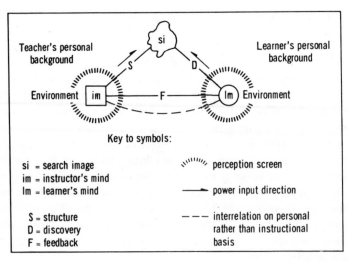

Fig. 4-2.

The components in this dialog are described and analyzed in other parts of the volume so let us define them here and refer to the place of the more complete description.

*The search image*—the immediate learning task in the system. For the purpose of this book it is in the cognitive domain. Defined and analyzed in Chapter 3.

*The instructor's mind*—the force responsible for the system as initiator and decision maker. Chapter 7 is devoted to a description and analysis of this part.

*The learner's mind*—the destination of the system. Chapters 6 and 10 go into detail on this part of the dialog. Chapter 10 will deal with the ways that these minds can affect the system.

*Structure*—the parts that make up the whole and their relation to each other. This concept is discussed fully in Chapter 5 and the teacher act in Chapter 8.

*Discovery*—the act of the learner in finding for himself the internal structure of the search image. Chapter 6 analyzes the process of discovery in the learner's mind.

*Feedback*—the phenomenon in the system that allows the instructor to correct his strategies so that the learner can work more accurately and profitably. Chapter 10 describes this more exactly and puts it into context.

*Perception screen*—the pattern of experiences and physiological background through which a mind perceives the world outside. This is discussed more fully in Chapter 10.

*Power input direction*—the emotional and intellectual power put into the system that makes the system operative. These are defined in Chapter 3 and discussed in Chapter 8 (teacher) and Chapter 6 (learner).

*Personal interrelation*—defines that part of the system beyond the mutual search for knowledge. In this area, the affective domain enters the system. Its influence on teacher strategy is discussed in Chapter 9.

**The Variations on the Theme.** Maintaining this dialog in a way that will bring about the best learning is the prime task of the instructor. It is not an easy job but perhaps the job would be made easier if we understand some of the factors that act on the system and, in acting upon it, vary it. There are four variables in the system that the teacher must understand and can, to some extent, control. These variables influence the instructor's decisions as he works with the system. Each of them is of importance and further chapters will describe and analyze them separately. These four variations are:

(1) the ordering of the knowledge

(2) the strategies for instruction

(3) the actions of minds on an idea

(4) the T-factor—the influence of time on the system.

These are given their order by their susceptibility to manipulation by the instructor. Variation (1) is far more readily managed than the others and each becomes successively more difficult for the instructor to control.

So the theme has been described and a model for it has been established. We turn now to a second cycle that further develops the thematic structure.

# THE THEME DEVELOPED

# chapter FIVE

# The Instruction of a Subject

> . . . to know what postulate of joy men have tried
> to live by, in sunlight and moonlight, until they died.
> —ROBERT PENN WARREN in the New Yorker.

As Stevenson said, the "final end of all true education is . . . wisdom which enhances learning, dignifies human relations, and plays, with a benign tolerance, over the follies and shortcomings of all God's children"; the final end of instruction is the search for meaning—the knowing of the postulates of joy that men have tried to live by. In the dialog between youth and age, innocence and wisdom, that is instruction, this search becomes the guiding criteria for the choice of the subject and the pattern of instruction.

Psychologists, as well as poets, sense this purpose. Jerome Bruner makes the point with grace and clarity saying that the subject to be learned has to deal with . . .

> . . . the sense of drama, the mysterious device by which we represent most vividly the range of human condition. . . . I would urge that in fashioning the instruction design to give students a view of the different faces and conditions of man, we consider more seriously the use of this most powerful impulse to represent the human condition in drama and, thereby, the drama of the human condition.[1]

This search for meaning by examining the postulates of joy and the human condition gives a sense of destiny and dignity which shapes all the subjects of schooling, both the "useful" and the "ornamental," to borrow a phrase from Ben Franklin. This search for meaning, this examination of postulates of joy, can go a long way to move a person from innocence to wisdom. It is the journey to the threshold of the mind.

[1] Jerome Bruner, Toward a Theory of Instruction (Cambridge, Mass.: Harvard University Press, 1966), p. 162–163.

## THE PURPOSES OF INSTRUCTION

Philosophers also have made this point. Philip Phenix,[2] poses the postulate, "since education is a means of helping human beings to become what they can and should become, the educator needs to understand human nature. He needs to understand people in their actualities, in their possibilities, and in their idealities." He proposes that the philosophic answer is that "humans are beings that discover, create, and express meanings." The life of meaning is, in essence, the life of man.

**Meaning as a Purpose of Instruction.** In order to give a greater insight into that term, Phenix describes four dimensions of meaning.

The first dimension of meaning is *experience*. This is in the life of the mind, an inner life that has the quality of *reflectiveness*. Conscious thought acts as a "mediating process" between stimulus and response. Meaning is based on a reflective mediation. Meaning presupposes a basic duality in which a person is both himself and an observer of himself. It is this duality that enables a person to *know* anything because this reflective mediation gives him a perception of relationships based on this duality.

The second dimension of meaning is *rule, logic,* or *principle*. Meaning is differentiated into types that are distinguished by a characteristic form, defined by a particular logic or structural principle.

The third dimension of meaning is *selective elaboration*. There is a limitless variety of meanings from which a selection is made on the basis of significance; they have an "inherent power of growth and lead to the elaboration of the enduring traditions of civilization." The varieties correspond to the varieties of scholarly disciplines.

The fourth and final dimension of meaning is *expression*. Meanings are communicable through symbols. Each kind of meaning has its own kind of symbols and the symbols become necessary for the transmission of meaning from one to another.

These are dimensions of meaning, the essence of human nature, the aim of instruction. The task of educators, then, is to construct the structure of studies from those meanings that have been effective in the development of civilizations—the postulates of joy that men have tried to live by.

**The Product and the Process of Learning in the System of Instruction.** In the search for meaning the learner learns two different things simultaneously. He learns a product of knowledge as well as a process for its derivation. He learns the matter of history as well as the historian's method; the matter of science as well as the scientific method. So in this way the learner reaches to the Stevensonian definition of wisdom as "an attitude *to* the fact." This knowledge of the process becomes the insight into the meaning.

[2] Philip Phenix, *Realms of Meaning* (New York: McGraw-Hill Book Company, 1964), pp. 17–25.

Perhaps another set of definitions will shed some needed light here. In the product side of the learning there are three categories that can be defined as data, knowledge, and meaning. *Data* can be defined as raw, unrelated fact; *knowledge* is fact with relationships; and *meaning* is achieved when the knowledge takes on a valuation and therefore a significance. This content of the search image can be placed in the chart of elements of the parts of the system that is being structured throughout this volume and first appeared in Chapter 3. (Fig. 5-1).

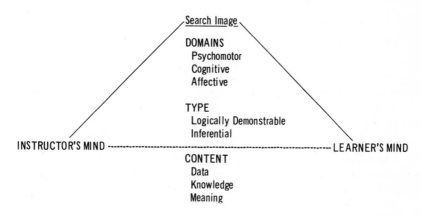

Fig. 5-1. Elements of parts of the system.

So the learner's search for meaning in the instructional dialog is enhanced when the instructor aims at a product of learning at the meaning level for the search image and in the examination of the search image leads the learner to the use of the inherent thought process.

**The Development of Rational Power as a Purpose of Instruction.** The idea of the process of knowledge as a legitimate aim of instruction has been given the imprimatur of the Educational Policies Commission in a volume published in 1961, *The Central Purpose of American Education*. In the words of the Secretary of that commission, James E. Russell, "hidden in it is a very profound revolution in American educational philosophy."[3]

According to the Commission, the central purpose of education is to develop the rational powers of every pupil. Students must develop the ability to think. They must know the process of knowledge. In the Commission's words:

> Thus the rational powers are central to all the other qualities of the human spirit. These powers flourish in a humane and morally respon-

[3] James E. Russell, *Universal Higher Education, Why and How*. Proceedings, Conference on Higher Education, 1965 (Harrisburg, Pa.: The Pennsylvania State Education Association, 1965).

sible context and contribute to the entire personality. The rational powers are to the entire human spirit as the hub is to the wheel.

These powers are indispensable to a full and worthy life. The person in whom—for whatever reason—they are not well developed is increasingly handicapped in modern society. He may be able to satisfy minimal social standards, but he will inevitably lack his full measures of dignity because his incapacity limits his stature to less than he might otherwise attain. Only to the extent that an individual can realize his potentials, especially the development of his ability to think, can he fully achieve for himself the dignity that goes with freedom.[4]

This development of the rational power is the *central purpose*, but there are other purposes as well.

> *Effective citizenship* is impossible without the ability to think. The good citizen, the one who contributes effectively and responsibly to the management of the public business in a free society, can fill his role only if he is aware of the values of his society. Moreover, the course of events in modern life is such that many of the factors which influence an individual's civic life are increasingly remote from him. His own firsthand experience is no longer an adequate basis for judgment. He must have in addition the intellectual means to study events, to relate his values to them, and to make wise decisions as to his own actions. He must also be skilled in the processes of communication and must understand both the potenialities and the limitations of communication among individuals and groups.

This has its roots in the famous *Cardinal Principles of Education* issued in 1918 which listed seven equal goals for education. This was reexamined in 1938 in the book of the Commission, *Purposes of Education in American Democracy*, which also adopted this pluralistic view to the goals of education. In 1961, the Commission declared that the development of the rational powers is central.

This was done in recognition of the role of change in our modern life and in the role of the mind in both causing the change and dealing with the changes.

**Knowledge as a Purpose of Instruction.** If the process of knowledge is justified on the grounds of the development of the rational power, what are the justifications of the product of knowledge? Bloom in *The Taxonomy of Educational Objectives*[5] points out that knowledge as an outcome of learning can be justified in many ways. "Perhaps the most common justification is that with increase in knowledge . . . there is a development of one's acquaintance with reality."

---

[4] The Educational Policies Commission, *The Central Purpose of American Education* (Washington, D.C.: The Commission, The National Education Association and The American Association of School Administrators, 1961), p. 6.

[5] Benjamin Bloom, ed., *The Taxonomy of Educational Objectives*, Handbook I (New York: David McKay Company, Inc., 1956), pp. 32–34.

Another justification is that knowledge is regarded as the basic tool or prerequisite for other aims. Knowledge becomes the material for the process or it is the test of the adequacy of the process.

Another justification is the rather socially derived one of the status of knowledge in our culture. "There is little doubt that our culture places tremendous weight on knowledge . . . as an important characteristic of the individual."

This duality of the purpose of instruction was neatly summed up in the annual report of the Carnegie Foundation in 1962:

> If we indoctrinate the young person in an elaborate set of fixed beliefs we are insuring his early obsolescence. The alternative is to develop skills, attitudes, habits of mind, in the kinds of knowledge and understandings that will be the instruments of continuous change and growth on the part of the young person. Then we shall have fashioned a system that provides for its own continuous renewal. This suggests a standard for judging the effectiveness of all education and, so judged, much education today is monumentally ineffective. All too often we are giving young people cut flowers when we should be teaching them to grow their own plants. We are stuffing their heads with the products of earlier innovation rather than teaching them how to innovate. We think of the mind as a storehouse to be filled rather than as an instrument to be used.[6]

The purpose of instruction, then, is to enable the student to learn how to learn so that the larger social enterprise of education can make itself felt on the individual.

## THE DOMAINS OF INSTRUCTION

Flowing from this purpose is, then, a defined area that becomes the subject to be studied in the process of instruction. Some years ago a group from the American Psychological Association met to try to develop a patterning of this subject matter and their work has been reported in *The Taxonomy of Educational Objectives*. Rather than classifying subject matter and content, they classified the "intended behavior of students—the ways in which individuals are to act, think or feel, as the result of participating in some unit of instruction."[7] They have three domains of their taxonomy and define them as:

> 1. *Cognitive*: Objectives which emphasize remembering or repro-ducing something which has presumably been learned, as well as objec-tives which involve the solving of some intellective task for which the

[6] Carnegie Corporation, *Annual Report* (New York: The Carnegie Corporation, 1962).

[7] Benjamin Bloom, *op. cit.*, p. 12.

individual has to determine the essential problem and then reorder given material or combine it with ideas, methods, or procedures previously learned. Cognitive objectives vary from simple recall of material learned to highly original and creative ways of combining and synthesizing new ideas and materials. . . . the largest proportion of educational objectives fall into this domain.

2. *Affective*: Objectives which emphasize a feeling tone, an emotion, or a degree of acceptance or rejection. Affective objectives vary from simple attention to selected phenomena to complex but internally consistent qualities of character and conscience. . . . such objectives . . . [are] expressed as interests, attitudes, appreciations, values, and emotional sets or biases.

3. *Psychomotor*: Objectives which emphasize some muscular or motor skill, some manipulation of material and objects, or some act which requires a neuromuscular coordination. . . . They are most frequently related to handwriting and speech and to physical education, trade, and technical courses.

The reader will undoubtedly recognize that such a threefold division is as ancient as Greek philosophy and that philosophers and psychologists have repeatedly used similar tripartite organizations: cognition, conation, and feeling; thinking, willing, and acting; etc. Modern research on personality and learning raises serious questions about the value of these simple distinctions.[8]

**The Cognitive Domain.** Of the three domains, the one most susceptible to the in-struction as we use the term is the cognitive domain. In this area the product-process duality is apparent; the cognitive domain is divided into two parts: on the one hand, knowledge and, on the other hand, abilities and skills. Of knowledge, the authors state:

Probably the most common educational objective in American education is the acquisition of knowledge or information. That is, it is desired that as the result of completing an educational unit, the student will be changed with respect to the amount and kind of knowledge he possesses. Frequently knowledge is the primary, sometimes almost the sole kind of, educational objective in a curriculum. In almost every course it is an important or basic one. By knowledge, we mean that the student can give evidence that he remembers, either by recalling or by recognizing, some idea or phenomenon with which he has had experience in the educational process. For our taxonomy purposes, we are defining knowledge as little more than the remembering of the idea of phenomenon in a form very close to that in which it was originally encountered.

This type of objective emphasizes most the psychological process of remembering. Knowledge may also involve the more complex processes of relating and judging, since it is almost impossible to present an individual with a knowledge problem which includes exactly the same stimuli, signals, or cues as were present in the original learning situation. Thus, any test situation involving knowledge requires some organization and reorganization of the problem to furnish the appropriate signals and

[8] David R. Krathwohl, *Taxonomy of Educational Objectives*, Handbook II, (New York: David McKay Company, Inc., 1964), pp. 6–7.

cues linking it to the knowledge the individual possesses. It may be helpful in this case to think of knowledge as something filed or stored in the mind. The task for the individual in each knowledge test situation is to find the appropriate signals and cues in the problem which will most effectively bring out whatever knowledge is filed or stored. For instance, almost everyone has had the experience of being unable to answer a question involving recall when the question is stated in one form, and then having little difficulty in remembering the necessary information when the question is restated in another form. This is well illustrated by John Dewey's story in which he asked a class, "What would you find if you dug a hole in the earth?" Getting no response, he repeated the question; again he obtained nothing but silence. The teacher chided Dr. Dewey, "You're asking the wrong question." Turning to the class, she asked, "What is the state of the center of the earth?" The class replied in unison, "Igneous fusion."

John Dewey's story also illustrates the rote recall nature of some knowledge learning. The emphasis on knowledge as involving little more than remembering or recall distinguishes it from those conceptions of knowledge which involve "understanding," "insight," or which are phrased as "really know," or "true knowledge." In these latter conceptions, it is implicitly assumed that knowledge is of little value if it cannot be utilized in new situations or in a form very different from that in which it was originally encountered. The denotations of these latter concepts would usually be close to what have been defined as "abilities and skills" in the taxonomy.

Whether or not one accepts this latter position, it is sufficient to note that knowledge by itself is one of the most common educational objectives. The most cursory reading of the standardized tests available or of teacher-made tests would indicate that tremendous emphasis is given in our schools to this kind of remembering or recall. A comprehensive taxonomy of educational objectives must, in our opinion, include all the educational objectives represented in American education without making judgments about their value, meaningfulness, or appropriateness. Knowledge, therefore, is one of our taxonomy categories.

The knowledge category in particular and, as noted earlier, the classifications of the taxonomy in general range from the simple to the more complex behaviors and from the concrete or tangible to the abstract or intangible. By simple we mean elemental, isolable bits of phenomena or information, e.g., "the capital of Illinois is Springfield," or "Arkansas contains much bauxite." Thus, our base subclassification is titled "knowledge of specific." At the upper end of the knowledge category the subclassifications refer to more complex phenomena. Thus, remembering a theory is a more complex task than remembering a specific such as the capital of a state. Knowledge of the theory of evolution, for instance, would be very complex. Accordingly, the subclassification at the complex end of the knowledge category is titled the "knowledge of theories and structures."

The knowledge categories may also be viewed as running from concrete to abstract. Thus, in general, knowledge of specifics will refer to concrete, tangible phenomena: "Insects have six legs;" "Most glass is brittle." But the more complex categories, as, for example, the name "knowledge of theories and structures" implies, tend to deal with abstract phenomena.

It might sometimes be useful for taxonomy purposes to distinguish knowledge with regard to the different specialties, fields of knowledge, or subdivisions of work in our schools. Thus, it would be possible to distinguish knowledge about the social sciences from knowledge about the physical sciences, and knowledge of physics from knowledge of chemistry, etc. Likewise, knowledge about man could be distinguished from knowledge about physical objects, etc. The taxonomy as developed here should be applicable to any of the subdivisions of knowledge or educational units in which school curricula are divided, but no attempt will be made to make all the possible applications or subdivisions in this Handbook. The reader may wish to develop such further classifications as are necessary for his work, using the taxonomy as a basis.

*What is knowable*

One of the major problems with regard to knowledge is determining what is knowable, for there are different ways in which something can be said to be known. Adding to this problem is the fact that different criteria of accuracy and authenticity are applied to knowledge in different areas, at least the knowledge to be learned in school. To a large extent knowledge, as taught in American schools, depends upon some external authority; some expert or group of experts is the arbiter of knowledge. Some information is the result of little more than convention and consensus. That is, a group of workers or experts in the field has come to some agreement on the ways in which particular terms will be defined, on the particular referents for selected symbols, or the most effective or practical ways in which lexicographers appear to make many arbitrary decisions in preparing a dictionary. The symbol for punctuation is solely a matter of convention. Memorizing the conjugation of verbs and the declensions of nouns is accepted as the proper approach to learning some foreign languages. Other information is known as the result of logical tests of consistency either by definition or by some logic of relationship. Certain kinds of geometry, mathematical propositions, and mathematical models are examples. Finally, some knowledge or information is known as the result of some historical, experiential, or pragmatic test. Thus, historical information is known as the result of a number of observations which are in agreement or which satisfy particular historical tests of their authenticity. Scientific information is known as a result of some observation, experiment, or test which meets the canons of scientific methodology.

It should also be noted that the validity, accuracy, and meaningfulness of information are relative in many ways and always related to a particular period of time. Thus, what is known in 1955 was not known in the same way in a previous era and will presumably undergo some changes in the future. Compare the way we pictured the atom twenty years ago with today's view of it.

There is also a geographical and cultural aspect to knowledge in the sense that what is known to one group is not necessarily known to another group, class, or culture. It must be clear from all this, that knowledge is always partial and relative rather than inclusive and fixed.[9]

[9] Benjamin Bloom, *op. cit.*, pp. 28–32.

The book defines the abilities and skills part of the cognitive domain as:

*The nature of abilities and skills*

Although information or knowledge is recognized as an important outcome of education, very few teachers would be satisfied to regard this as the primary or the sole outcome of instruction. What is needed is some evidence that the students can do something with their knowledge, that is, that they can apply the information to new situations and problems. It is also expected that students will acquire generalized techniques for dealing with new problems and new materials. Thus, it is expected that when the student encounters a new problem or situation, he will select an appropriate technique for attacking it and will bring to bear the necessary information, both facts and principles. This has been labeled "critical thinking" by some, "reflective thinking" by Dewey and others, and "problem solving" by still others. In the taxonomy, we have used the term "intellectual abilities and skills." The most general operational definition of these abilities and skills is that the individual can find appropriate information and techniques in his previous experience to bring to bear on new problems and situations. This requires some analysis or understanding of the new situation; it requires a background of knowledge or methods which can be readily utilized; and it also requires some facility in discerning the appropriate relations between previous experience and the new situation.[10]

**The Affective Domain.** The divisions into domains was an arbitrary decision that seems to be natural, yet there are areas of overlap. It is useful to view these domains as being on a continuum with a shading from one into another rather than to view them as three compartments. Krathwohl does make an interesting distinction as they relate to the school.

In the cognitive domain we are concerned that the student shall be able to do a task when requested. In the affective domain we are more concerned that he *does do* it when it is appropriate after he has learned that he *can do* it. Even though the whole school system rewards the student more on a *can do* than a *does do* basis, it is the latter which every instructor seeks. By emphasizing this aspect of the affective components, the affective domain brings to light an extremely important and often missing element in cognitive objectives.[11]

Morally, the question arises as to whether or not, in a society dedicated to freedom of the individual, it is right to structure a system of values. Ethical right demands that each individual be allowed to make up his own mind as to values and subsequent modes of conduct. Therefore the instruction system has the right, and in a deep sense, the duty, to present the individual with the alternatives of behavior and leave him free to choose his own pattern. This becomes a moral dilemma of the highest order. Sometimes it resolves

[10] *Ibid.*, p. 38.
[11] David R. Krathwohl, *op. cit.*, p. 60.

itself into simple terms: "What do I do about a student who knows all of the facts about Hitler, passes the tests (in the cognitive domain) with a straight A, and then says that Hitler was a good man. Does he get an A in the course?"

In examining this question of teaching in the affective domain, Edwin Fenton[12] helps to resolve this dilemma by defining three types of values: behavioral, procedural, and substantive. He believes that the schools have a right to teach the first two but have no right to teach the last. He defines the first two in this way:

> A behavioral value concerns procedure in the classroom. We teachers are retained by the board of education to instruct the young, and we are paid for doing our jobs. We cannot tolerate students who disrupt classes or who make our bookkeeping unnecessarily complicated by coming to school late day after day. In order to perform adequately as teachers, we must enforce certain rules of order in the classroom. Students must keep quiet when others have the floor; they must keep textbooks in good condition; they must not molest their classmates; they must not defenestrate the teacher. Each teacher has a right to teach and enforce a value system that implies these patterns of behavior. If he does not teach such values he will be unable to teach. Not only must he tell students that these values are good ones, he must also enforce rules which these values imply, even to the extent of sending Jane or Johnny to the office where they speak harshly and carry big sticks. I am prepared to defend the proposition that every teacher ought to teach behavioral values. If he does not he cannot teach effectively.
>
> I am also prepared to defend the proposition that we ought to teach procedural values. Critical thinking is better than uncritical thinking; this canon underlies the entire scholarly world. If a student insists that his prejudices should not be challenged and defends them with an emotional appeal, he should be *forced* to subject them to the test of evidence and to defend them in the face of the full array of scholarly argument. In science classes we have a right to insist that students accept the method of experimentation as preferable to what "common sense" might tell them. In mathematics they *must* accept the structure of the deductive method. In history and the social sciences they must be willing to look at evidence for their position and to accept the method by which social scientists and historians arrive at conclusions. Unless parents and school officials give us the right to teach the validity of certain procedural values, we cannot teach our disciplines.

If the schools have no right to teach substantive values, may they then bring them into the school? Fenton makes the necessary distinction here; rather than teaching values, the school should teach *about* values. He puts this persuasively:

> Let me illustrate what I mean about the distinction between teaching values and teaching about values. If a teacher teaches substantive

[12] Edwin R. Fenton, *Teaching the New Social Studies* (New York: Holt, Rinehart & Winston, Inc., 1966), pp. 42–45.

values about government, he may tell his students that democracy is better than totalitarianism. If he teaches about values, he raises questions about democracy and totalitarianism. He might ask students to define the objectives a government should set for itself. Then he might ask what alternative ways men have devised for attaining these objectives and insist that students examine the logical consequences of these alternatives. The goal of this procedure is not unanimous agreement; it is to persuade each student to examine goals and means for himself in order to arrive at a political philosophy by which he can guide his later life. If a student does not alter a value, this process ought to provide him with evidence to support a position he may have held as a mere prejudice. If he does change a value judgment, he has scrapped an opinion that failed to meet the test of evidence and adopted a sounder one. In either case he is better off.

**The Criteria for Selection.** The next logical step in this argument is that, if we have a product and a process to be learned and because it is impossible to teach every bit of knowledge, we must find some criteria for selection of the knowledge to be taught. Selecting criteria for choice of knowledge has been a task for many thinkers in the field of education.

Philip Phenix, looking at instruction, gives four principles for selection which focus on the knowledge.

> Four principles for the selection and organization of content are suggested as means of ensuring optimum growth in meaning. The first principle is that the content of instruction should be drawn entirely from the fields of *disciplined inquiry*. The richness of culture and the level of understanding achieved in advanced civilization are due almost entirely to the labors of individual men of genius and of organized communities of specialists. A high level of civilization is the consequence of the dedicated service of persons with special gifts for the benefit of all. Every person is indebted for what he has and is to a great network of skilled inventors, experimenters, artists, seers, scholars, prophets, and saints, who have devoted their special talents to the well-being of all. Nobody, no matter how capable, can make any perceptible progress on his own without dependence on the experts in the various departments of life.
>
> It follows that the teacher should draw upon the specialized disciplines as the most dependable and rewarding resource for instructional materials. While he should seek to make the disciplined materials his own, he should not presume to originate the knowledge to be taught, nor should he expect the fruits of learning to come forth as if by miracle from the shared experience of the students or as the products of common sense.
>
> This term "discipline" is not meant to refer to an unchanging set of established fields of knowledge. New disciplines are regularly coming into being, such as cybernetics, parapsychology, theory of games, astronautics, and the like. New combinations, such as biochemistry and history of science, are forming. Also, many established disciplines are undergoing radical internal transformations: modern physics, music, history, and theology, to mention only a few. In fact, there is scarcely a field of study that is not today different in important respects from what it was

only a few decades ago. Hence the present proposal to use materials from the disciplines does not constitute an argument for education to return to a traditional subject-matter curriculum. It simply argues for the exclusive use of materials that have been produced in disciplined communities of inquiry by men of knowledge who possess authority in their fields. Given the developments in disciplined inquiry, the proposal to use knowledge from the disciplines favors a modern rather than a traditional type of curriculum.

The second principle for the selection of content is that from the large resources of material in any given discipline, those items should be chosen that are particularly *representative* of the field as a whole. The only effective solution to the surfeit of knowledge is a drastic process of simplification. This aim can be achieved by discovering for each discipline those seminal or key ideas that provide clues to the entire discipline. If the content of instruction is carefully chosen and organized so as to emphasize these characteristic features of the disciplines, a relatively small volume of knowledge may suffice to yield effective understanding of a far larger body of material. The use of teaching materials based on representative ideas thus makes possible a radical simplification of the learner's task.

A third and related principle is that content should be chosen so as to exemplify the *methods of inquiry* and the modes of understanding in the discipline studied. It is more important for the student to become skillful in the ways of knowing than to learn about any particular product of investigation. Knowledge of methods makes it possible for a person to continue learning and to undertake inquiries on his own. Furthermore, the modes of thought are far less transient than are the products of inquiry. Concentration on methods also helps to overcome the other two forms of meaninglessness earlier considered, namely, fragmentation and surfeit of materials. Every discipline is unified by its methods, which are the common source of all the conclusions reached in that field of study. As this common thread, the characteristic modes of thought are included in the category of representative ideas, which, as indicated above, allow for the simplification of learning.

A fourth principle of selection is that the materials chosen should be such as to arouse *imagination*. Growth in meaning occurs only when the mind of the learner actively assimilates and re-creates the materials of instruction. Ordinary, prosaic, and customary considerations do not excite a vital personal engagement with ideas. One of the qualities of good teaching is the ability to impart a sense of the extraordinary and surprising so that learning becomes a continuous adventure. According to this principle, ordinary life-situations and the solving of everyday problems should not be the basis for curriculum content. The life of meaning is far better served by using materials that tap the deeper levels of experience. Such materials reveal new perspectives on old problems by throwing familiar experiences into fresh combinations and showing old beliefs in novel contexts. Such imaginative use of materials generates habits of thought that enable the student to respond to rapid changes in knowledge and belief with zest instead of dismay and to experience joy in understanding rather than the dead weight of ideas to be absorbed and stored.[13]

[13] Philip Phenix, *op. cit.*, pp. 10–12.

The psychologist Bruner, focusing on the learning, lists four principles for selection.

> The first has to do with what is taught. It would seem, from our consideration of man's evolution, that principal emphasis in education should be placed upon skills—skills in handling, in seeing and imaging, and in symbolic operations, particularly as these relate to the technologies that have made them so powerful in their human expression. . . .
>
> This brings us immediately to a second conclusion. It relates literally to the meaning of the word *curriculum*, a word that derives from a course to be run. It is perhaps a wrong word. A curriculum should involve the mastery of skills that in turn lead to the mastery of still more powerful ones, the establishment of self-reward sequences.
>
> The third conclusion relates to change. If there is any way of adjusting to change, it must include, as we have noted, the development of a metalanguage and "metaskills" for dealing with continuity in change.
>
> Finally, it is plain that if we are to evolve freely as a species by the use of the instrument of education, then we shall have to bring far greater resources to bear in designing our educational system.[14]

And finally, the educationist, Benjamin Bloom, focusing on the teaching-learning process adds his four principles.

> Four decisions to be made with respect to the nature of the knowledge objectives included in the curriculum should be noted. These relate to "How much knowledge should be required learning?"; "How precisely need the student learn the required knowledge?"; "How is knowledge best organized for learning?"; and "How meaningful need required knowledge-learning be to the student?"[15]

## THE IN-STRUCTION OF A PRODUCT

For an examination of the relation of the certainty of knowledge to the system of instruction, we turn again to Bruner's ideas.

In the article "After John Dewey, What," Bruner states flatly that, ". . . the structure of knowledge—its connectedness and the derivations that make one idea follow from another—is the proper emphasis in education."[16]

This idea of importance of structure to education was first enunciated in the seminal volume *The Process of Education*. In this short book, which has had a great effect on recent educational thought, the concept of structure in knowledge is examined.

Defining the concept, Bruner states, ". . . grasping the structure of a subject is understanding it in a way that permits many other things to be

[14] Jerome Bruner, *Toward a Theory of Instruction*, pp. 34–37.

[15] Benjamin Bloom, *op. cit.*, p. 36.

[16] Jerome Bruner, *On Knowing, Essays for the Left Hand* (Cambridge, Mass.: Harvard University Press, 1962), p. 120.

related to it meaningfully. To learn structure, in short, is to learn how things are related."

Emphasizing the structure of knowledge in the system of instruction gives these advantages, according to Bruner:

> Good teaching that emphasizes that structure of a subject is probably even more valuable for the less able student than for the gifted one, for it is the former rather than the latter who is most easily thrown off the track by poor teaching.
>
> Mastery of the fundamental ideas of the field not only involves the grasping of general principles, but also the development of an attitude toward learning and inquiry, toward guessing and hunches, toward the possibility of solving problems on one's own.
>
> *     *     *
>
> The study of the structure makes the subject more interesting.
>
> The study of the structure makes the subject more comprehensible.
>
> The study of the structure slows forgetting of the subject.
>
> The study of the structure "narrows the gap between 'advanced' and 'elementary' knowledge."[17]

Relating meaning to structure, Joseph Schwab says,

> It need hardly be added that if meaning is lost by the absence of the structure appropriate to a body of knowledge, that meaning is seriously distorted by replacing the appropriate structure by some other structure. Yet, in the past twenty years, we have worked and revised any number of subject matters in order to fit them to the bed of views about how and when and under what circumstances this or that is most readily learned. It would be well if, in future, we thought twice before we modified an item of knowledge in order to fit it to a psychological structure. alien to it.[18]

**Disciplines as the Container of the Structure.** Coming right down to the classroom operation within this idea of the structure of knowledge, we come up against the question of wherein is the structure contained. The answer, the subject matter, is too facile. King and Brownell, writing on theories of curriculum make an important distinction:

> The distinction between *disciplined knowledge,* as used in this book, and *subject matter,* as this term has come to be defined by schoolmen in the first half of this century, must be made clear. The former means the disciplined substance and artful syntax of bodies of thoughtful men; the latter signifies the atomistic, unrelated, factual material which

---

[17] Jerome Bruner, *The Process of Education* (Cambridge, Mass.: Harvard University Press, 1961), p. 7 *et passim.*

[18] In Stanley Elam, ed., *Education and the Structure of Knowledges* (Chicago: Rand McNally & Company, 1964), pp. 36–37. This book is an interesting example of the influence of the concept of "structure" on education. It is a report of a symposium "to try to think through the meaning of the expression, to analyze the concept for which the expression stands and to see what bearing, if any, the concept of knowledge structure has upon education and teaching."

has been presented according to an inappropriate theme, or worse, as a potpourri. Subject matter in this sense has been the bane of students and teachers in schools and colleges since the dawn of formal education. We do not advocate a return to "traditional" pedagogy. On the contrary, we propose a new conception of curriculum which makes the long-standing educational argument between *child-centeredness* and *subject matter* unnecessary and unproductive. The fulfillment of each person's capacity for meanings through encounters with the significant realms of experience is the most humane of educational ideas.[19]

Phenix, in discussing the disciplines as a source for the structure makes the same point, ". . . the present proposal to use materials from the disciplines does not constitute an argument for education to return to a traditional subject-matter curriculum. It simply argues for the exclusive use of materials that have been produced in disciplined communities of inquiry by men of knowledge who possess authority in their fields."[20]

**The Process and the Product and the Medium and the Message.** A warning has been sounded lately for those engaged in constructing theories of knowledge and the transmission of knowledge and information. Marshall McLuhan in two books, *The Gutenberg Galaxy* (1962) and *Understanding Media* (1964), hypothesizes that, while our conscious attention is on the content of knowledge, we are also accepting, and to him docilely, the impact of the media that carries the content. It is his point that for several generations knowledge and information have been in a linear, sequential pattern forced by the media of the printed word, frozen into lines of words by Gutenberg's invention. In the present day, modern man is under the impact of media of a much greater complexity in radio and particularly television. Thus the idea of sequential thought and linear patterns may have to be reconstructed. McLuhan offers little toward any reconstruction, but his warning should be heeded.

## THE IN-FORMING OF A PROCESS

The search for meaning in the system of instruction suggests that it might be found in the product of knowledge and the process of knowledge. Fresh looks have been given to this latter of late, and the new look seems to be summed up in the phrase "inquiry." This implies a free examination of the subject along lines of thought that lead to the learner's own discovery of the process and the product.

This concern with the process hasn't been particularly new; the science of pedagogy rests on it. There have been many terms for it over the years: problem-solving, critical thinking, the investigative method, the reflective

---

[19] Arthur King and John Brownell, *The Curriculum and the Disciplines of Knowledge* (New York: John Wiley & Sons, Inc., 1966), p. 94.

[20] Philip Phenix, *op. cit.*, p. 11.

method, to name the outstanding ones. But be that as it may, an emphasis on process by any name is sweet if that process results in a student's learning.

This thought process seems to take place within a certain mental set that can be added to the chart of elements of the parts of the system that is being built in this volume. These are sensate, lingual-symbolic, and emotive. When the search image is in the psychomotor domain, the mental set of the learner is sensate; his physical senses are used. He physically acts out his learning. When the search image is in the cognitive domain, the mental set becomes symbolic, and usually the symbol is that of language. So his learning search and result is expressed in arrangement of symbols. If the search image is in the affective domain, the mental set is emotive. His learning is expressed through his emotions. That is to say, the outside world sees the results of his learning through his emotional acts. (See Fig. 5-2.)

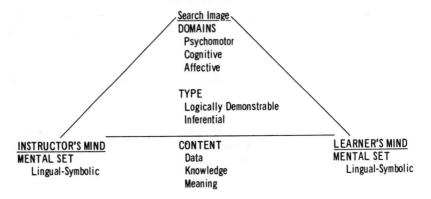

FIG. 5-2. Elements of parts of the system.

Any analysis of this idea quickly shows, of course, the difficulty of categorization. Lines between cognitive and affective learning blur. This makes the moral dilemma of instruction in the affective domain, discussed above, even more poignant.

**Analytic and Intuitive Approaches.** In the cognitive and the affective domains, the thought processes of the learner fall into two broad patterns: analytical and intuitive.[21] Mentioning that it is unclear what constitutes intuitive understanding, Bruner maintains that we can distinguish it as

. . . we can distinguish between inarticulate genius and articulate idiocy —the first represented by the student, who, by his operations and conclusions, reveals a deep grasp of subject but not much ability to "say how

[21] The terms, as well as the discussion, are drawn from Chapter 4 of Bruner's, *The Process of Education*. However, other terms can be used for the same idea, e.g., "algorithmic" and "heuristic." Martin Heidigger in his *Discourse on Thinking* speaks of them as "calculative" and "meditative."

it goes," in contrast to the student who is full of seemingly appropriate words but has no matching ability to use the ideas for which the words presumably stand.

Too often the instructor's aim seems to be to produce learners of the latter variety, the memorizers of appropriate words, the articulate idiots.

Analytic thought processes have been analyzed and intuitive thought processes have been thought about intuitively. One conclusion is that the two processes are complementary. Using intuitive thinking, an individual may arrive at an end that can be, in turn, checked by an analytical process.

Another conclusion is that it is difficult to identify intuitive ability by observable behavior. If we could, then the intuitive pattern would be an analytic one.

There are some variables that affect intuitive thinking. Bruner[22] raises a series of conjectures about this. What variables seem to affect intuitive thinking?

Is the development of intuitive thinking in students more likely if their teachers think intuitively? Perhaps simple imitation is involved, or perhaps more complex processes of identification. It seems unlikely that a student would develop or have confidence in his intuitive methods of thinking if he never saw them used effectively by his elders. The teacher who is willing to guess at answers to questions asked by the class and then subject his guesses to critical analysis may be more apt to build those habits into his students than would a teacher who analyzes everything for the class in advance.

Does the providing of varied experience in a particular field increase effectiveness in intuitive thinking in that field? Individuals who have extensive familiarity with a subject appear more often to leap intuitively into a decision or to a solution of a problem—one which later proves to be appropriate. . . . Implicit in this emphasis, it appears, is the belief that understanding of structure enables the student, among other things, to increase his effectiveness in dealing intuitively with problems.

What is the effect on intuitive thinking of teaching various so-called heuristic procedures? A heuristic procedure, as we have noted, is in essence a nonrigorous method of achieving solutions of problems. While heuristic procedure often leads to solution, it offers no guarantee of doing so. An algorithm, on the other hand, is a procedure for solving a problem which, if followed accurately, guarantees that in a finite number of steps you will find a solution to the problem if the problem has a solution. Heuristic procedures are often available when no algorithmic procedures are known; this is one of their advantages. Moreover, even when an algorithm is available, heuristic procedures are often much faster. . . .

The student who becomes obsessively aware of the heuristic rules he uses to make his intuitive leaps may reduce the process to an analytic one. On the other hand, it is difficult to believe that general heuristic rules— the use of analogy, the appeal to symmetry, the examination of limiting conditions, the visualization of the solution—when they have been used frequently will be anything but a support to intuitive thinking.

[22] Jerome Bruner, *Process of Education*, pp. 61–66, *et passim*.

Should students be encouraged to guess, in the interest of learning eventually how to make intelligent conjectures? Possibly there are certain kinds of situations where guessing is desirable and where it may facilitate the development of intuitive thinking to some reasonable degree. There may, indeed, be kind of guessing that requires careful cultivation. Yet, in many classes in school, guessing is heavily penalized and is associated somehow with laziness. Certainly one would not like to educate students to do nothing but guess, for guessing should always be followed up by as such verification and confirmation as necessary; but too stringent a penalty on guessing may restrain thinking of any sort and keep it plodding rather than permitting it to make occasional leaps. May it not be better for students to guess than to be struck dumb when they cannot immediately give the right answer? . . .

Should we give our students practice not only in making educated guesses but also in recognizing the characteristics of plausible guesses provided by others—knowing that an answer at least is of the right order of magnitude, or that it is possible rather than impossible? It is our feeling that perhaps a student would be given considerable advantage in his thinking, generally, if he learned that there were alternatives that could be chosen that lay somewhere between truth and complete silence. But let us not confuse ourselves by failing to recognize that there are two kinds of self-confidence—one a trait of personality, and another that comes from knowledge of a subject. It is no particular credit to the educator to help build the first without building the second. The objective of education is not the production of self-confident fools. . . .

Finally, what can be said about the conditions in which intuitive thinking is likely to be particularly effective? In which subjects will mastery be most aided by intuitive procedures followed by checking? Many kinds of problems will be best approached by some combination of intuitive and other procedures, so it is also important to know whether or not both can be developed within the same course by the same teaching methods.

The intuitive leap, the shrewd guess, nonanalytic thinking can be encouraged but, says Bruner,

> . . . the pedagogic problems in fostering such a gift are severe. . . . For one thing, the intuitive method . . . often produces the wrong answer. It requires a sensitive teacher to distinguish an intuitive mistake—an interestingly wrong leap—from a stupid or ignorant mistake, and it requires a teacher who can give approval and correction simultaneously to the intuitive student.[23]

**The Process of Discovery.** Thought processes should reach an end, and in the system of instruction the end is learning. We know that the learner learns best when he discovers the learning for himself. This, of course, does not mean that he discovers something new to the world, but he discovers it new to himself. To him, it has just the same joy whether it is new to him

[23] *Ibid.*, p. 68.

or to the world. Bruner defines these four benefits as:

(1) The increase in intellectual potency
(2) The shift from extrinsic to intrinsic rewards
(3) The learning of the heuristics of discovering
(4) The aid to conserving memory.

The hypothesis that he poses concerning the increase in intellectual potency is that

> emphasis on discovery in learning has precisely the effect on the learning of leading him to be a constructionist, to organize what he is encountering in a manner not only designed to discover irregularity and relatedness, but also to avoid the kind of information drift that fails to keep account of the uses to which information might have to be put. Emphasis on discovery, indeed, helps the learner to learn the varieties of problem solving, of transforming information for better use, helps him to learn how to go about the very task of learning.[24]

So Bruner points out in this particular regard that the benefit of learning through discovery is the process of discovery as well as the product.

In reference to the extrinsic and intrinsic motives, Bruner states that to the degree that one is able to approach learning as the task of discovering something rather than learning about it, to that degree there will be a tendency for the child to work with the autonomy of self-reward or more properly be rewarded by discovery in itself. He goes on to warn that learning that starts in response to the rewards of parental or teacher approval or to the avoidance of failure can too readily develop a pattern in which the child is seeking clues as to how to conform to what is expected of him. In other words, too often the system of instruction produces the type of learner mind that is working through extrinsic motivations, whose idea of problem solving is to solve the problem of what the teacher wants rather than what the subject demands.

The third benefit to be derived from learning by discovery is what Bruner calls the heuristics of discovery. The hypothesis here is that "it is my hunch that it is only through the exercise of problem solving and the effort of discovery that one learns the working heuristics of discovery. The more one has practiced, the more likely one is to generalize what one has learned into a style of problem solving or inquiry that serves for any task encountered." He goes on to warn that what is unclear is the kinds of training and teaching that produce the best effects. This is where the experimentation in teaching must take place now. But he does believe that one of the ways of coming to this art of inquiry and to learning by discovery is by a careful study of the subject matter that is formally structured, a study that takes place in a logical thought process.

---

[24] Jerome Bruner, *On Knowing*, p. 87. *et passim.*

The final benefit in the process of discovery is the aid to conserving memory. Bruner maintains that the "problem of human memory is not storage but retrieval." The process of memory, then, is the process of problem solving. The problem becomes one of organizing and "placing" material in the memory in such a way that it can easily be retrieved on call. The material that is the most accessible is organized in patterns along the lines of a person's own interests and cognitive styles. It is most likely to be placed along the ordinary routes of intellectual travel used as one searches his own memory bank. Thus, says Bruner, "the very attitudes and activities that characterize . . . discovering . . . seem to have the effect of conserving memory."

## SUMMARY

**The Role of Inquiry.** Looking at the social enterprise of instruction after his years as Commissioner of Education, Francis Keppel[25] wrote of the role of inquiry in the learning of knowledge:

> Knowledge takes a greater meaning if it has been gained through struggle and self-questioning rather than through passive acceptance.
> To establish inquiry posed three assumptions:
> 1. Students must have an intellectual challenge by bringing them into direct and repeated confrontation with the gaps and inadequacies in their knowledge and understanding, both to incite their curiosity and to invite them to search for ideas and principles that explain the data they are trying to relate.
> 2. Students need access to raw data and to the ideas of others by bringing the learner close to the world outside. This implies more exposure to uninterpreted things, places, people and documents.
> 3. Inquiry demands independence. Schools have to offer freedom to gather and process data. This implies setting aside timetables of content coverage.

This, then, is the source for the search image in the system of education—the structure of knowledge. Along with the structure of knowledge as the product is the process of derivation of that knowledge. Parallel to the process of derivation is the process of thought of the learner, analytical and intuitive. So, from a discussion of the product and process, let us turn to another part of the system—the learner.

## SUGGESTED READINGS

Ford, G. W., and Lawrence Pugno. *The Structure of Knowledge and the Curriculum* (Chicago: Rand McNally & Company, 1964).

[25] Francis Keppel, *The Necessary Revolution in American Education* (New York: Harper & Row, Publishers, 1966), p. 116.

GAGNE, ROBERT M. "The Learning Requirements for Enquiry," *Journal of Research in Science Teaching* (January, 1963), pp. 144–153.

PARKER, J. CECIL and LOUIS RUBIN. *Process as Content: Curriculum Design and the Application of Knowledge* (Chicago: Rand McNally & Company, 1966).

# chapter SIX

# Instruction of Students

*Youth is a wonderful thing. What a crime it is to waste it on children.*—GEORGE BERNARD SHAW.

"I don't teach a subject. I teach people," runs a cliché that mirrors a little more sentiment than actuality. "You can always tell a _____ student, but you can't tell him much," (you supply the name of the school for the blank) runs another rueful cliché of the blue room in many a school. And Shaw sums up with careful thought and customary levity the whole mystery of that part of the system of instruction that furnishes the learning mind. For the learning student in America is at once mystifying, fascinating, and frightening. He begs to be understood and withstands understanding. He will outnumber his elders in a few years and educators have debated long and loud over how to handle him.

## THE MANAGEMENT-CONTENT BALANCE IN INSTRUCTION

Often this debate has centered around the point of how much attention should be placed on the subject to be learned (both product and process) and how much on the shaping of the learner. This has ballooned into the rather fruitless argument over the amount and proportion of "methods courses" v. "subject matter" courses in a teacher's training. Because this type of argument quickly slides off into an *ad hominem* realm, there are vigorous ascriptions of fallibility by the professors of one course to the professors of the other. Time, patience, and our appointed task keep us from a further exploration of these latter points but Conant, in his work on the education of teachers, covered the subject straightforwardly and with a weary dispassion that seemed to show the argument was rather senseless.[1]

No sensible person would argue for his subject to the exclusion of con-

---

[1] James B. Conant, *The Education of American Teachers* (New York: McGraw-Hill Book Company, 1963).

cern on how to present it nor vice versa. So the question, as so often happens, revolves around the middle between the poles, where there is gray matter between the black and the white.

To picture this necessary balance let us look at it in the charted fashion shown in Fig. 6-1.

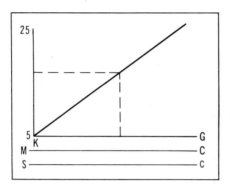

Fig. 6-1.

The vertical line represents the chronological age of learners in the formal system of instruction in the United States; the horizontal line represents the graded categories from kindergarten (K) to graduate school (G). The diagonal line is the balance line. Below the horizontal axis are two continua: the upper represents the presentation and is bounded by management (M) on one end and content (C) on the other.[2] The lower continuum is the curricular organization and is bounded by social gain (S) and cognitive gain (C).

To find the balance, a line is drawn from whatever age is selected to the balance line. From that point of intersection a vertical line is dropped to the horizontal axis. When this line is extended to the continua, the "proper" balance between the poles is indicated.

For purposes of illustration we have used the poetic sweet sixteen age. The line shows that the point of emphasis is somewhat beyond the midpoint with a greater emphasis on the content than on management and with greater emphasis on a subject-centered curriculum than on a pupil-centered. This means that, generally speaking, in deciding upon a presentation pattern for the learner in that age and grade group there is slightly more emphasis on content to be learned than on management concerns. It also means that the curricular content shall be centered more on cognitive gain for the learner than social gain.

This demonstrates the unique and, in a way, untidy position of the

[2] Management, in this sense, focuses attention on the physical side of the classroom situation as opposed to the method of organizing the content.

secondary teacher in the schools. This model shows graphically that he has to be acquainted with and be able to handle both ends of the continuum.

At the one extreme of kindergarten the instruction emphasis is completely on the pupil. When the instructor sees a child with a dreamy look on his face that means that his mind is in another world; she is bound to probe this and switch her approach so that the dreams will be in focus on the work at hand. Often she will stop the whole process of instruction to converse with the dreamer.

"Willie, what are you thinking about?"

"I was jes' thinkin' of the fight I seen this mornin'."

"Was it a bad fight?"

"There wuz cops 'n' everthin'. She hit him and he. . . ."

At this point the system becomes therapy as the teacher, sensing Willie's need for a purgation of the emotions, works with him to the detriment of his learning about community helpers.

However, the imagination boggles at accepting the idea of a professor in a graduate class interrupting the probing of some esoteric knowledge to attentively hear out a daydreamer. In the first levels, the social gain must be served; at the last levels the cognitive gain.

Also, if little Willie, working away in his first grade of school, doesn't break through to the proper understanding, the teacher repeats with many variations until he does learn; there is a shift in methods that demands that the teacher be well versed in that area.

Conversely, at the other limits of the formal schooling, if young William does not get it the first time round, he probably won't get another chance, for the instructor and class have most likely moved on to another point. The subject is central, and the instructor must be competent in that.

In a rough sort of way, teacher education programs seem to recognize this balance so that kindergarten teachers have quite a bit of methodology in their training whereas the instructor slated to teach in higher education generally has very little or none in a formal way.

This balance means that the instructor must have an insight into the psychological and sociological workings of his learners in order to have a rational basis for the instruction that he will do.

## PSYCHOLOGICAL BACKGROUNDS OF STUDENTS

Not quite like Gaul, all students are divided into two parts (for our purposes): the psychological, which is the student as an individual, and the sociological, which is the student as a member of a social body. The psychological background has two points for our purposes: one is learning and the other is thinking.

**Learning Processes.** Learning is a process having three complete parts: the acquisition, the transformation, and the evaluation. These three parts form themselves into a learning episode.[3] Acquisition means the absorbing of information that is either new information or that is replacement for that which is already held. Transformation means to find the relationships within that new information to the old information, and lastly the evaluation is the acceptance or the internalization of it. Now, interestingly enough, the phases of this pattern can go on almost simultaneously. A student, or a listener, or a learner, acquires information. Immediately that information is taken into his mind where it is related to known information and immediately evaluated. These three stages have manifestations in personal behavior that can and must be noted by the instructor. At the acquisition phase, it seems that the student manifestation is often anxiety. The first step in a learning episode often results in the sense of dropping from a cliff into the unknown. When a learner comes running up to the teacher and says, "What do you want me to do?" or "I am not sure what you want me to do here," he is manifesting anxiety. When the teacher hands a task to a student to do in a very formal assignment or just in a question, a frown or a squirm can show that anxiety. Some psychologists say that no learning will take place without this initial anxiety. Therefore, an instructor has to remember that if he is not engendering a sense of anxiety in his students he is not teaching. At the very least he should not be amazed and upset at any anxiety that he does arouse.

The transformation period may be roughly analogous to a gestation period. Manifestations of this in a pupil's behavior are often such statements as "I don't know" or "I am still thinking" or something of that nature. It isn't that he is basically stupid; he may have leanings in that direction, but it's just that he is thinking it over. He is going through a period of transforming, relating these particular learnings to his past experiences and learnings. Often the first response is a little bit awkward, a little bit searching, and apt to be off in many directions. This is not to be condemned; this period of gestation doesn't bring about the most graceful mental activity immediately. That grace comes through polishing and experience. The vagueness of this often shows itself in the question-and-answer exercises that characterize so much of the instructional dialog. Frequently the teacher asks a question with the specificity of "What do you think of the world today?" or something rather "narrow" like that. Then he stands amazed that he doesn't get a ready answer.

The final stage, evaluation, is the acceptance or rejection of the knowledge. If the learner does accept it, of course, there is an internalization that results in a change in behavior (which is one definition of learning).

[3] Jerome Bruner, *The Process of Education* (Cambridge, Mass.: Harvard University Press, 1961), p. 48 *et passim*.

These three stages seem to form a cycle for learning that should be accounted for in the system of instruction. Through the feedback mechanism in the system, the instructor becomes sensitive to the episodic nature of this cycle and regulates the teaching episodes to the learning episodes.

Another phenomenon about learning patterns has to be considered by the instructor: this is the span of attention of a learner—the length of time that he can be attentive to a task. This is, of course, such an idiosyncratic affair, dependent upon each situation, that it becomes impossible to generalize in writing about it. But merely because it is difficult to generalize adequately does not mean that it is unimportant to the system of instruction. Again, this becomes another factor to be judged in the feedback system. Generally speaking (we shall attempt the impossibility of generalizing) the attention span of youth to a specific verbal learning task can be around ten minutes. Thus new learnings in the same structure and new activities will have to be employed to pick up where a previous attention span has left the learner.

Another factor enters the learning picture here. One of the cardinal principles of the instruction process is that individuals are different. And each class is composed of different individuals with different capacities to learn and different rates of learning and different attention spans. This matter of the differences of the individual becomes another variation that the instructor has to remember as he works with the system of instruction.

**Thought Processes.** Learning is a process whereby knowledge is acquired, transformed, and evaluated. Then, for that stored knowledge to achieve utility, it must enter into the learner's behavior pattern. In short, it must become the tools for his thinking. Learning about learning is difficult, thinking about thinking is even more difficult, and trying to draw a line between learning and thinking is well nigh impossible. If it is possible, it can be done on the level of definition of the two processes, the wholes and the parts.

A few years ago some basic thinking took place in this realm in order to classify, codify, and otherwise categorize what instruction could do. The resultant *Taxonomy of Educational Objectives*[4] has had a marked effect on thought about instruction. This work neatly defines these thought process in this way:

1.00 KNOWLEDGE

Knowledge, as defined here, involves the recall of specifics and universals, the recall of methods and processes, or the recall of a pattern, structure, or setting. For measurement purposes, the recall situation involves little more than bringing to mind the appropriate material. Although some alteration of the material may be required, this is a rela-

[4] Benjamin Bloom, ed., *The Taxonomy of Educational Objectives*, Handbook I (New York: David McKay Company, Inc., 1956), p. 201–207.

tively minor part of the task. The knowledge objectives emphasize most the psychological processes of remembering. The process of relating is also involved in that a knowledge test situation requires the organization and reorganization of a problem such that it will furnish the appropriate signals and cues for the information and knowledge the individual possesses. To use an analogy, if one thinks of the mind as a file, the problem in a knowledge test situation is that of finding in the problem or task the appropriate signals, cues, and clues which will most effectively bring out whatever knowledge is filed or stored.

1.10 KNOWLEDGE OF SPECIFICS
The recall of specific and isolable bits of information. The emphasis is on symbols with concrete referents. This material, which is at a very low level of abstraction, may be thought of as the elements from which more complex and abstract forms of knowledge are built.

    1.11 KNOWLEDGE OF TERMINOLOGY
    Knowledge of the referents for specific symbols (verbal and non-verbal). This may include knowledge of the most generally accepted symbol referent, knowledge of the variety of symbols which may be used for a single referent, or knowledge of the referent most appropriate to a given use of a symbol.

        To define technical terms by giving their attributes, properties, or relations.
        Familiarity with a large number of words in their common range of meanings.

    1.12 KNOWLEDGE OF SPECIFIC FACTS
    Knowledge of dates, events, persons, places, etc. This may include very precise and specific information such as the specific date or exact magnitude of a phenomenon. It may also include approximate or relative information such as an approximate time period or the general order of magnitude of a phenomenon.

        The recall of major facts about particular cultures.
        The possession of a minimum knowledge about the organisms studied in the laboratory.

1.20 KNOWLEDGE OF WAYS AND MEANS OF DEALING WITH SPECIFICS
Knowledge of the ways of organizing, studying, judging, and criticizing. This includes the methods of inquiry, the chronological sequences, and the standards of judgment within a field as well as the patterns of organization through which the areas of the fields themselves are determined and internally organized. This knowledge is at an intermediate level of abstraction between specific knowledge on the one hand and knowledge of universals on the other. It does not so much demand the activity of the student in using the materials as it does a more passive awareness of their nature.

    1.21 KNOWLEDGE OF CONVENTIONS
    Knowledge of characteristic ways of treating and presenting ideas and phenomena. For purposes of communication and consistency, workers in a field employ usages, styles, practices, and forms which best suit their purposes and/or which appear to suit best the phenomena with which they deal. It should

be recognized that although these forms and conventions are likely to be set up on arbitrary, accidental, or authoritative bases, they are retained because of the general agreement or concurrence of individuals concerned with the subject, phenomena, or problem.

Familiarity with the forms and conventions of the major types of works, e.g., verse, plays, scientific papers, etc.

To make pupils conscious of correct form and usage in speech and writing.

1.22 KNOWLEDGE OF TRENDS AND SEQUENCES

Knowledge of the processes, directions, and movements of phenomena with respect to time.

Understanding of the continuity and development of American culture as exemplified in American life.

Knowledge of the basic trends underlying the development of public assistance programs.

1.23 KNOWLEDGE OF CLASSIFICATIONS AND CATEGORIES

Knowledge of the classes, sets, divisions, and arrangements which are regarded as fundamental for a given subject field, purpose, argument, or problem.

To recognize the area encompassed by various kinds of problems or materials.

Becoming familiar with a range of types of literature.

1.24 KNOWLEDGE OF CRITERIA

Knowledge of the criteria by which facts, principles, opinions, and conduct are tested or judged.

Familiarity with criteria for judgment appropriate to the type of work and the purpose for which it is read.

Knowledge of criteria for the evaluation of recreational activities.

1.25 KNOWLEDGE OF METHODOLOGY

Knowledge of the methods of inquiry, techniques, and procedures employed in a particular subject field as well as those employed in investigating particular problems and phenomena. The emphasis here is on the individual's knowledge of the method rather than his ability to use the method.

Knowledge of scientific methods for evaluating health concepts.

The student shall know the methods of attack relevant to the kinds of problems of concern to the social sciences.

1.30 KNOWLEDGE OF THE UNIVERSALS AND ABSTRACTIONS IN A FIELD

Knowledge of the major schemes and patterns by which phenomena and ideas are organized. These are the large structures, theories, and generalizations which dominate a subject field or which are quite generally used in studying phenomena or solving problems. These are at the highest levels of abstraction and complexity.

1.31 KNOWLEDGE OF PRINCIPLES AND GENERALIZATIONS

Knowledge of particular abstractions which summarize observations of phenomena. These are the abstractions which are of value in explaining, describing, predicting, or in determining the most appropriate and relevant action or direction to be taken.

Knowledge of the important principles by which our experience with biological phenomena is summarized.

The recall of major generalizations about particular cultures.

1.32 KNOWLEDGE OF THEORIES AND STRUCTURES

Knowledge of the *body* of principles and generalizations together with their interrelations which present a clear, rounded, and systematic view of a complex phenomenon, problem, or field. These are the most abstract formulations, and they can be used to show the interrelation and organization of a great range of specifics.

The recall of major theories about particular cultures.

Knowledge of a relatively complete formulation of the theory of evolution.

## INTELLECTUAL ABILITIES AND SKILLS

Abilities and skills refer to organized modes of operation and generalized techniques for dealing with materials and problems. The materials and problems may be of such a nature that little or no specialized and technical information is required. Such information as is required can be assumed to be part of the individual's general fund of knowledge. Other problems may require specialized and technical information at a rather high level such that specific knowledge and skill in dealing with the problem and the materials are required. The abilities and skills objectives emphasize the mental processes of organizing and reorganizing material to achieve a particular purpose. The materials may be given or remembered.

2.00 COMPREHENSION

This represents the lowest level of understanding. It refers to a type of understanding or apprehension such that the individual knows what is being communicated and can make use of the material or idea being communicated without necessarily relating it to other material or seeing its fullest implications.

2.10 TRANSLATION

Comprehension as evidenced by the care and accuracy with which the communication is paraphrased or rendered from one language or form of communication to another. Translation is judged on the basis of faithfulness and accuracy, that is, on the extent to which the material in the original communication is preserved although the form of the communication has been altered.

The ability to understand non-literal statements (metaphor, symbolism, irony, exaggeration).

Skill in translating mathematical verbal material into symbolic statements and vice versa.

2.20 INTERPRETATION

The explanation or summarization of a communication. Whereas translation involves an objective part-for-part rendering of a communication, interpretation involves a reordering, rearrangement, or a new view of the material.

The ability to grasp the thought of the work as a whole at any desired level of generality.

The ability to interpret various types of social data.

### 2.30 EXTRAPOLATION

The extension of trends or tendencies beyond the given data to determine implications, consequences, corollaries, effects, etc., which are in accordance with the conditions described in the original communication.

The ability to deal with the conclusions of a work in terms of the immediate inference made from the explicit statements.

Skill in predicting continuation of trends.

### 3.00 APPLICATION

The use of abstractions in particular and concrete situations. The abstractions may be in the form of general ideas, rules of procedures, or generalized methods. The abstractions may also be technical principles, ideas, and theories which must be remembered and applied.

Application to the phenomena discussed in one paper of the scientific terms or concepts used in other papers.

The ability to predict the probable effect of a change in a factor on a biological situation previously at equilibrium.

### 4.00 ANALYSIS

The breakdown of a communication into its constituent elements or parts such that the relative hierarchy of ideas is made clear and/or the relations between the ideas expressed are made explicit. Such analyses are intended to clarify the communication, to indicate how the communication is organized, and the way in which it manages to convey its effects, as well as its basis and arrangement.

### 4.10 ANALYSIS OF ELEMENTS

Identification of the elements included in a communication.

The ability to recognize unstated assumptions.

Skill in distinguishing facts from hypotheses.

### 4.20 ANALYSES OF RELATIONSHIPS

The connections and interactions between elements and parts of a communication.

Ability to check the consistency of hypotheses with given information and assumptions.

Skill in comprehending the interrelationships among the ideas in a passage.

### 4.30 ANALYSIS OF ORGANIZATIONAL PRINCIPLES

The organization, systematic arrangement, and structure which hold the communication together. This includes the "explicit" as well as "implicit" structure. It includes the bases, necessary arrangement, and the mechanics which make the communication a unit.

The ability to recognize form and pattern in literary or artistic works as a means of understanding their meaning.

Ability to recognize the general techniques used in persuasive materials, such as advertising, propaganda, etc.

5.00 SYNTHESIS

The putting together of elements and parts so as to form a whole. This involves the process of working with pieces, parts, elements, etc., and arranging and combining them in such a way as to constitute a pattern or structure not clearly there before.

> 5.10 PRODUCTION OF A UNIQUE COMMUNICATION
>> The development of a communication in which the writer or speaker attempts to convey ideas, feelings, and/or experiences to others.
>>> Skill in writing, using an excellent organization of ideas and statements.
>>> Ability to tell a personal experience effectively.

> 5.20 PRODUCTION OF A PLAN, OR PROPOSED SET OF OPERATIONS
>> The development of a plan of work or the proposal of a plan of operations. The plan should satisfy requirements of the task which may be given to the student or which he may develop for himself.
>>> Ability to propose ways of testing hypotheses.
>>> Ability to plan a unit of instruction for a particular teaching situation.

> 5.30 DERIVATION OF A SET OF ABSTRACT RELATIONS
>> The development of a set of abstract relations either to classify or explain particular data or phenomena, or the deduction of propositions and relations from a set of basic propositions or symbolic representations.
>>> Ability to formulate appropriate hypotheses based upon an analysis of factors involved, and to modify such hypotheses in the light of new factors and considerations.
>>> Ability to make mathematical discoveries and generalizations.

6.00 EVALUATION

Judgments about the value of material and methods for given purposes. Quantitative and qualitative judgments about the extent to which material and methods satisfy criteria. Use of a standard of appraisal. The criteria may be those determined by the student or those which are given to him.

> 6.10 JUDGMENTS IN TERMS OF INTERNAL EVIDENCE
>> Evaluation of the accuracy of a communication from such evidence as logical accuracy, consistency, and other internal criteria.
>>> Judging by internal standards, the ability to assess general probability of accuracy in reporting facts from the care given to exactness of statement, documentation, proof, etc.
>>> The ability to indicate logical fallacies in arguments.

> 6.20 JUDGMENTS IN TERMS OF EXTERNAL CRITERIA
>> Evaluation of material with reference to selected or remembered criteria.
>>> The comparison of major theories, generalizations, and facts about particular cultures.

Judging by external standards, the ability to compare a work with the highest known standards in its field—especially with other works of recognized excellence.

These definitions can serve as choices by the instructor as he selects search images that fulfill his aims—they can give direction to the system. These objectives then become the thought processes of the learner and are manifested through a learner verbal behavior. They can be placed in the chart of elements of the parts of the system as shown in Fig. 6–2. They

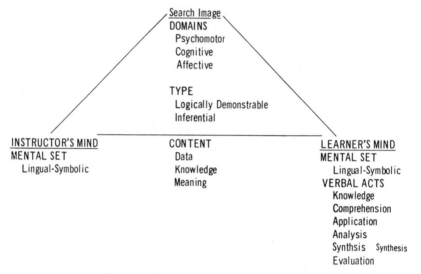

Fig. 6-2. Elements of parts of the system.

are placed in this chart in a way that suggests the incremental pattern that seems to be inherent. That is to say, that to get to the thought process of evaluation the other thought processes seem to be involved to one degree or another.

**The Motivation to Learn.** The other side of the learning act is the power that impels the student to learn. The power that the student puts in the system is this motivation. This is the impulse to reach up to the search image to acquire it, to transform it, to evaluate it, to learn about it.

This motivation, again, has its parts worthy of examination.[5] The most obvious type of motivation is extrinsic. This extrinsic motivation means that the student receives a sense of purpose from an exterior source rather than from within the person himself. This is the motivation that says, "I am learning this today to pass the test on Friday to get a grade at the end of

[5] These thoughts are drawn from Jerome Bruner, *Toward a Theory of Instruction* (Cambridge, Mass.: Harvard University Press, 1966), Chapter 6.

the term which will go in with other grades for the other courses and result in a diploma, and that diploma will open doors for me in society that couldn't be opened for me before. So the reason I'm in your course, Buster, at all, is to get the grade to get the diploma to get out of here."

Teachers can use extrinsic motivation as these examples show:

When the teacher says, as he so often does, "Pay attention or you will miss this for the test on Friday."

When the teacher says, "If you don't behave you will go down to the principal's office where you will assume a certain position and receive two good swats in the presence of three signatories or witnesses or whatever the legal procedure is."

When the teacher says to a small child, "Come on now, you ought to behave better than that or they will think you are the wrong type of kid."

Intrinsic motivation means that there is something inherent within the subject to be learned that will drive the learner toward the learning of it. There are some characteristics about the human mind apparently that seem to work toward this intrinsic motivation.

The first is *curiosity*. The human is born with a sense of trying to find out what's going on. As time goes on and as the child develops, his sense of curiosity is channeled. Sometimes it is pretty well conditioned out of him, but nevertheless he is curious. He wants to find out what things are going on and how he can best learn those things. Some way or another the system must capitalize on his sense of curiosity and it appears tactically that the best way to capitalize on this sense of curiosity in the high school student is to once again urge him into being curious. Perhaps the job is to revive his spirit of exploration by setting up a task in such a way that he feels a necessity of just finding something out for its own sake. Perhaps the epitome of this intrinsic motivation is displayed by the man who climbed to the top of the mountain "because it's there." His curiosity compelled him to get to the top of the mountain. Curiosity compels a person to do something just because it is there to be done, because it might matter a little that he got it done.

Anatole France went to the heart of this when he said, "The whole art of teaching is only the art of awakening the natural curiosity of young minds for the purpose of satisfying it afterwards."

This sense, then, that it might matter leads us to the second human characteristic apparent here. (This becomes a very optimistic statement about the human condition.) This is the drive to be *competent*; a drive to achieve a degree of expertness about a task. If we are beginning to note now in human behavior that humans do want to be competent, the conflict comes on the value determination of what it is in which they would like to be competent. One of Hell's Angels roaring on his motorcycle is trying his best to be competent in his way. He might be at odds with society because society tends to reject people who go 65 miles an hour in 35-mile-an-hour zones and get caught at it, but he is nevertheless trying to be competent. The classroom is the scene of this conflict often. A learner is accused by the instructor of "not trying," "not being interested." But the trouble may be so simple as the fact that he is just marching to a different drum from that which the teacher is beating for him.

How does this drive affect teaching? It has been noticed that this drive for competence must depend on the task's having a certain worth to it and a certain organization to it. It must have a beginning and an end; something that can be seen, something that can be totaled in the mind of the learner. The learner begins to see that the sense of curiosity leads him to a specific task, a specific search image. Then his drive for competence moves him to absorb and learn. To be brought to its greatest fruition, what he has to learn must be a capsule; it must be a totality that he can grasp.

As this sense of curiosity and drive to competence move the learner, another phenomenon comes into play: massed practice vs. spaced practice. In the learning process an interrupted task will be learned better when the student returns than if he had not been interrupted. In this drive to competency we find that to achieve that competence an interruption can be helpful. Those of a more poetic nature would perhaps rather call this the "daisy-picking" effect. This may alleviate guilt feelings of those who have been frustrated in a drive toward a goal and thrown it over and then gone out to pick a daisy or watch the world go by or just kick something.

If this effect is of such value, how can it be introduced into the system? The instructor can capitalize on natural breaks in the structure-discovery dialog. These will give the same effect on students if somehow or another there is built into this structure a time for reflection, a time for relaxation, a time for getting away from the whole thing, a time for daisy picking. Then come back to the subject at hand. This can be done very straight-forwardly in the middle of a class period by having a break. It can be done in very narrow terms—speaking chronologically—in the midst of presentation of a concept by a joke or a bit of relaxation or just by a mere transfer of the physical presence from one corner of the room to the other. The artful instructor soon learns this matter of pacing.

A third characteristic that seems to be an impelling force in the human in the learning process is that he tends to identify with some sort of *model*. In the classroom the learner will therefore tend to behave like the instructor. Bruner notes this and warns that what the teacher must be

> . . . to be an effective competence model, is a day-to-day working model with whom to interact. It is not so much that the teacher provides a model to *imitate*. Rather, it is that the teacher can become part of the student's internal dialogue—somebody whose respect he wants, someone whose standards he wishes to make his own. It is like becoming a speaker

of a language one shares with somebody. The language of that interaction becomes a part of oneself, and the standards of style and clarity that one adopts for that interaction become a part of one's own standards.[6]

(It could be noted by any doubters that this point of modeling is reinforced by the old truism in education that teachers teach as they have been taught rather than as they should teach.)

The teacher is a model for the learner on two levels. One is the apparent level of physical patterns. The learner will behave physically in the same manner that the teacher behaves. He will model his behaviors on those of the teacher. This, however, is not identification, a term that generally describes a relationship with a good deal more emotional attachment.

The other level is the intellectual level. The instructor holds a valuable resource, a desired competence that is attainable by interaction. These are what Bruner terms "competence models." The learner often adopts a tryout-correction-revision procedure to attain the model that is being held up. In this case the model is the instructor's intellectual behavior as well as the search image that is in the system. This becomes the theoretical rationale for the idea of the search image in the system of instruction.

The fourth of these intrinsic motivations is *reciprocity*—the idea that the human mind in learning has a deep need to react with another mind and operate in a reciprocal arrangement toward a mutually established goal. This becomes the theoretical rationale behind our premise that instruction is a dialog.

But there are two rather important ramifications and repercussions of this reciprocal dialog in the instructional system. If the teacher wishes to capitalize on this reciprocity, it must be remembered that he is in a reciprocal relationship with a group of individuals in the dialog. His class becomes a series of unilateral dialogs of varying degrees of intensity. The second ramification grows from this. The system must establish and protect the different individuals in this system. Each operates differently, each views the world through his own perception screen. Each assumes a different role in the group. To capitalize on these differences enhances the feeling of reciprocity in the class. A give-and-take relationship between the instructor and learner ensues rather than the more rigid pattern of "I have the message and I shall pass it on to you."

In the psychological background of the students, therefore, the elements that have the most pertinence to the system for instruction are the motivations that impel the student to learn. Our society establishes extrinsic motivations, often in the sense of rewards and punishments. Learners also bring to the system intrinsic motives: curiosity, search for a model, the need for competence, the need for reciprocity. To these motivations of the learners we must add another ingredient here. It is not so much an addition as it is

[6] *Ibid.*, p. 45.

a reminder. In Chapter 5 we discussed the in-structuring or in-forming of knowledge in the learner's mind and, with the idea that the best way for this to happen was through a process of inquiry on the learner's part, a process that would result in discovery's taking place. This discovery is of the structure of the search image; its parts and their relationships and how the parts fit the whole.

This gets us at the heart of the system for instruction. Through this process of inquiry, the learner is motivated in the best way, the way that will bring about the deepest learning both of a product and a process.

But there is more to the background of the learner than the psychological. From an examination of him as a learning individual, let us turn to an examination of him as a member of a group and see what difference to the system that makes.

## SOCIOLOGICAL BACKGROUNDS FOR INSTRUCTION

Anyone who has been caught up in the happy pastime of people-watching (a game with many adherents, complex rules as yet unwritten, and odd rewards) is impressed with the fact that the human spirit comes in a wide, wide variety of packages and manifests itself in myriad ways. This is a rather unorthodox description of the idea of individual differences among the learners. Each is different, each must be treated differently.

But there are certain commonalities. They derive from the common social background which in our culture is called adolescence.

**The Phenomenon of Adolescence.** The term "phenomenon" is used advisedly. One of the characteristics of this period of life that has become a life in itself that has been noted[7] is that it is not a natural state of development through which all of the human animals must pass. Perhaps because it is in a life period wherein puberty has its onset, there is a temptation to view it as a time of puberty. Deeper probing and reflection reveals that this is a life period peculiar to the youth in only the industrialized sections of the world societies. More time is needed to train the youth to take their place in these societies, more skills are needed that demand older minds and bodies. Younger persons become a threat to older persons in the work force. All of these are reasons that youth is set aside for a few years.

Less complex societies do not have this period and do not even have a word for it in their language.[8] Children proceed directly into adulthood often performing tasks along with the older members of society when they are in the age period of 5–10. If there is any initiation into adulthood, it

[7] Wilhelm Tenbruck, "Contemporary Adolescence," *Diogenes* (December, 1961).

[8] Margaret Mead's *Coming of Age in Samoa* (New York: The New American Library of World Literature, Inc., 1949) is a classic work on "growing up" as practiced in more "primitive" societies. Chapter 14, "Education for Choice," compares that society with the North American society and is particularly pertinent.

comes in puberty rites rather than during adolescence. (Of course this is not to say that adolescence in our present culture is not one long puberty rite. We must save examination of this interesting postulate for other times and other places.) An indication of this industrial derivation of the idea of adolescence comes from an examination of patterns of living of youth in developing societies. In Brazil, for instance, the youth in the middle and upper classes of the industrializing cities live a modern adolescent life while in the interior of the country in the rural, pastoral areas youth are not adolescent; they are younger adults.

Another characteristic of adolescence is that it is a period marked by instability, insecurity, and impulsiveness. These derive from many sources. The young are set apart from society into a period of preparation for a society that is rather unknown to them. They sense this as an in-between time; they catch the hint from a society that says, on the one hand, "You're old enough to know better," and moments later, "Stop it, you're not old enough." This is a time of trying on styles, looking for enduring patterns, and at the same time discarding styles with a speed that makes one wonder if anything can last for any time.

There is a circularity in operation here. These are living, breathing humans who, at times, have been known to think. With a sense of confusion, compounded with conformity and a striving to please, the teen-ager, to be normally a teen-ager, dons the cloak of the abnormal. A young girl turning thirteen gleefully announces, "I'm a teen-ager; now I can have problems." A young boy kisses his mother and she, shocked by the fact that this has never happened before, is calmed when she finds out that he, too, has been reading her copy of a book on adolescence and found that young boys fall in love with their mothers. The book set up a pattern for a syllogism: "I am a normal young boy. Normal young boys love their mothers. Therefore. . . ."

These same sociologists note another characteristic about adolescence. The period is being extended in societies. The age of entering it is lowering (from 13 to 8 or 9) the age of leaving it rising (from 18 to 25). This thought is often unsettling and/or unacceptable to those who are, in Shaw's phrase, "towering in the confidence of twenty-one." Add this to the fact of the growth of numbers of teen-agers in our society and we can see that adolescence as a phenomenon is going to be with us in ever-growing force.

This growth takes on new dimensions when it takes place in a society whose members seem to be dedicated to staying young. In a society where mothers try more to look like their daughters, where the new breed (the young Turk) gets the laurels, where rewards are reserved for those who think young, there is a grave danger of society's accepting as a common denominator of behavior the instability, insecurity, and impulsiveness of adolescence. In this society, innocence does not grow into wisdom; it often changes into psychological trauma.

Finally, the last characteristic grows out of these. Adolescence becomes a culture that is almost separate and unique. It has its own language, its own customs, and its own mores. It is a cohesive culture that resists intrusions as many a teacher has found when he tries, to his dismay, to speak the language or adopt the customs.

Adolescence is more than a state; it is something other than a period. It is also a process. Edgar Friedenberg[9] points out that

> . . . adolescence is a stage in life in which every human being must come to terms with his own being, his own divergence, and the meaning of his relationship to other individuals. . . . *Self-definition is the prime developmental task of adolescence*; indeed, it is the process of adolescence itself. [Italics added.]

It is small wonder that "a boy's will is the wind's will, and the thoughts of youth are long, long thoughts." The process of self-definition takes place in this subculture that has a strange place in our society. It must also be said that this process is a saving grace of adolescence to those who dream of its ending in maturity and wisdom.

Friedenberg points out that "adolescents are among the last social groups in the world to be given the full nineteenth-century colonial treatment." He admits that the colonial analogy is defective, saying that "the essence of the 'teen-ager's' status is that he is in transition; the essence of the native's status is that he is not supposed to be." What results is that "the plight of the adolescent is basically similar to that of an emigrant in that he can neither stay what he was nor become what he started out to be."

Society has a rather ambivalent attitude toward the youngsters in this stage and this process. On the one hand it is trying to "induce them to abandon their barbarism and assimilate the folkways of the normal adult life." In this attitude society seems to urge the teen-ager through the process, telling him to hurry up and become adult.

At the same time, on the other hand, society reinforces the stage by wooing "the dimply, pimply set."[10] A concerted effort is made to entice the buying power of the teen-ager in the United States. This is not inconsiderable; the 25 million between 13 and 19 are estimated to spend 18 billion dollars per year and by 1970 the predicted 30 million of that age group will have disposable incomes totaling 30 billions of dollars. In addition to this direct buying power, teen-agers are said to have an influence over the spending of 35 billions more each year as they help to shape the buying habits of their families. This is just the threshold of their buying power; they are, at the end of their teen years, just starting a lifetime of consumer-

[9] Edgar Friedenberg, *Coming of Age in America* (New York: Random House, Inc., 1965), p. 218.

[10] Charles and Bonnie Remsburg, "Wooing the Dimply Pimply," *New York Times Magazine* (June 5, 1966), p. 100.

ship. Half of the young women will become wives before they are 20 and more will have their first child at 19 than any other age. So they have a large impact on the economy now and represent an even greater potential.

Interestingly enough, the schools are coming to be used as a locale for influencing this buying power and for building consumer purchasing habits. Manufacturers send out teaching aids that display their product, and merchandisers look to the schools and the students for tips on what styles and tastes will hit and which will not.

It is impossible to consider the place of the adolescent in society without considering the setting for so much of his activity, the school. The school is the field in which this process takes place. Friedenberg assesses the school in this way:[11]

> Our ideological commitment to equality of opportunity implies to us that the school is obligated to devote itself to a continuous search on behalf of that equality, while defining opportunity in such a way as to place it beyond the reach of privilege. It prevents us from seriously considering that any individual or special group may make us richer simply by being what it is. Yet, adolescence is a stage of life in which every human being must come to terms with his own being, his own divergence, and the meaning of his relationship to other individuals. The meanest and most-cringing sycophant, the blandest and slyest bureaucrat, were closer to being human in adolescence than they were ever to become again. Self-definition is the prime developmental task of adolescence; indeed, it is the process of adolescence itself. The animus directed against the "inward" and the "subjective" is directed against such elements in all youth. But these are the elements that make adolescence possible, and that lead to *personal* growth and maturity, to acceptance of life as a unique and momentous sequence of actively monitored experiences, each contributing to the richness and relevance of the next.

If this is the ideal, Friedenberg points out that we are falling short:

> I have found the life of the high school to be, in this respect, very often like a bad book; sentimental, extrinsically motivated, emotionally and intellectually dishonest. The animus is directed against those of the young who are too fully alive, too completely realized, to fit among its characters. They are disparaged; by its disparagement the school wastes its opportunity to help youngsters create a style suited to their romantic age. The essential first step in encouraging growth in adolescents is surely to link their new sexual energy and their occasionally flamboyant quest for identity to the meaningful larger aspects of past and present culture, which is what taste means and disciplined self-expression requires. If the baroque manifestations of adolescence elicit instead an attitude of sulky oppression . . ., the adolescent is thrown back upon resources he has not yet developed. The school then grudgingly supports the numerous more conformist and emotionally dependent youth within the youth culture itself against the occasional youth who retains his exuberance; using them to help isolate him and deny him the only valid source of

[11] Edgar Friedenberg, *op. cit.,* p. 218 *et passim.*

status; recognition that his actions and his work express a personal view of reality, for which only he can be responsible. In his ensuing despair, the school helps him—helps him to become assimilated within the "teenage culture." In a little while, it is as if he had never been.

What does this mean? In another part of the book Friedenberg[12] provides an answer:

> . . . The school endorses and supports the values and patterns of behavior of certain segments of the population, providing their members with the credentials and shibboleths needed for the next stages of their journey, while instilling in others a sense of inferiority and warning the rest of society against them as troublesome and untrustworthy. In this way, the school contributes simultaneously to social mobility and social stratification. It helps to see to it that the kinds of people who get ahead are those who will support the social system it represents; while those who might, through intent or merely by their being, subvert it are left behind as a salutary moral lesson.

As a consequence of this attitude of the school and of the adolescent within the school, Friedenberg found that many times the whole adolescent pattern was to cooperate with the system. So apparently the school, as defined in his study, is exercising some shaping power over the adolescents; it is not sinking into an adolescent anarchy. It remains for deeper study than we can give here to determine whether the directions the school does shape are the best for the society and what it stands for.

## CONFLUENCE OF PSYCHOLOGICAL AND SOCIOLOGICAL BACKGROUND

The adolescents in high schools today are individuals in whom reside drives, motives, and ambitions that are derived from within themselves and from their society in a web that is impossible to unravel. So, to see how the psychological and the sociological come together in classroom operation, let us examine one group within the school, the academically able.[13] Though the able compose only a small percentage of the total adolescents in the schools, they are worthy of study because they probably will become tomorrow's leaders. Also, and more to the point, they are most often held by society and the schools to be the models for all of the others. The school and the society will accept the fact that there are differences and that some don't measure up to these models but implicit is the idea that the differences are in degree, not in kind.

There are four types of these able adolescents, the high-achieving studious (about 60%), the social leaders (about 20%), the creative intellectuals (about 20%), and the rebels (a small percentage).

---

[12] *Ibid.*, p. 49.
[13] Elizabeth Drews, "The Four Faces of Able Adolescents," *Saturday Review* (January 19, 1963).

The high-achieving studious are attuned to what parents and schools, and particularly schools, expect. They tend to conform to what teachers demand or to what teachers suggest. Since teachers' expectations are more often than not at odds with the dominant teen-age culture, this means that these students generally put their school work ahead of pleasure. If given the choice between what the adolescent culture demands and what the teacher demands, they take what the teacher demands. That's why they are high achievers, because, what does the teacher do? Rewards them for copying themselves after the teacher. He says, "Aha, there must be nothing greater in the world than somebody who is trying to be like me. Hey, I am the model." That's why they get their high achievement scores. They are generally not the school leaders. They are not particularly creative and original. They are highly productive in quantitative terms, and not too productive in creative terms.

Another type of able adolescent is the social leader. The social leaders tend to conform more to what the teen-age group wants than to what the teacher wants. But they have enough innate curiosity, drive and ability to be able students though not precisely in the terms that the teacher does want. Their parents are often young and handsome, well educated, and well connected. Their basic values are materialistic, rounded out with hedonism, but they temper their competitiveness with good-humored togetherness. They are a particularly handsome looking group, the boys and the girls alike, and they set the taste for the culture. These are the social leaders. The boys from this group are on the athletic squads.[14] The girls are the cheerleaders and the editors and the presidents, and both are the students voted most likely to succeed in the culture.

There is a third group that is called the creative intellectuals. These creative intellectuals have a certain pattern. They tend to receive lower grades because they tend to go beyond what the teacher wants. They tend to become prickly types of kids and they tend to get below the surface and quite often below the belt in some of the questions that they ask of the teacher. They are often brighter than the teacher, as a matter of fact, and they take no pains to hide it. One student spent a year reading Ibsen and Freud simultaneously and assiduously applied Freudian theory to Ibsen passages. Drews quotes another as saying, "I read all of Freud and Shakespeare this year and lots of other stuff besides, and I am so busy educating myself that I just don't have time to get more than a B in my school work."

The first type did what the teacher wanted, the second one what the adolescent group wanted, the third what he wanted. Finally, there is a fourth type—the rebel. He does what nobody wants. He just rebels against

[14] John Updike's novel *Rabbit, Run* offers a dramatic view of the not-so-able social leader and his problems of coping with his world out of high school.

society. The rebels are low in achievement, and their hallmark is noncon-formity. His behavior could be called individualistic, creative, nonintellectual. They reject, are rejected by, teachers and other students and are probably cordial in their reciprocation. However, they are often leaders in a sub-culture outside of school.

Perhaps the non-able, run-of-the-mill general student differs from the able in the expressions of ability, but there probably is quite a common pattern throughout all the ability levels as to the sources of their motivation. In all groups there must be many who get their drives from the teacher and the system, some who get them from the mass of students, and some who get them from within themselves. It is probable that the percentages shift for the general students with more getting their motivations from the group, fewer from the schools, and fewest from within themselves in the creative sense of that term.

These students are not necessarily stable within these categories. There is much evidence to show that they do change and in predictable ways. To demonstrate this, Drews offers the chart shown in Fig. 6–3.

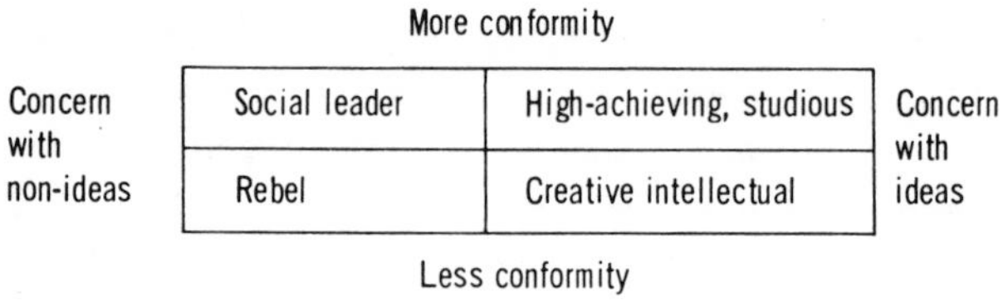

More conformity

| Concern with non-ideas | Social leader | High-achieving, studious | Concern with ideas |
|---|---|---|---|
| | Rebel | Creative intellectual | |

Less conformity

FIG. 6-3.

The movement is likely to be in a vertical or a horizontal plane. But it is hardly conceivable that the rebel would become a high-achieving student or vice versa or that the social leader would become the creative intellectual or, even more unbelievable, the creative intellectual become the social leader.

## SUMMARY

The system of instruction must meet this challenge of adolescents reach· ing for self-definition, a *sine qua non* for wisdom. In finding a balance be-tween method and content, in understanding the psychological backgrounds and the sociological backgrounds of his students, the instructor could well keep in mind as a model the autonomous individual who is manifested by the release of three capacities:

Awareness: the capacity to see a coffee pot and hear the birds sing in one's own way and not the way one has been taught. To live in the here and now, not the elsewhere, past or future.

Spontaneity: the freedom to choose and express one's feelings from all the assortment available.

Intimacy: spontaneous, game-free candidness of an aware person.[15]

It is very difficult to say how it can be done, but a wise woman with a warm heart, one of that unheralded troop that guards against the night on the battlements of the quiet corners of this world, once said that maturity must support youth on an open hand, hoping to have the wisdom to know when to close the fist.

## SUGGESTED READINGS

COLEMAN, JAMES. *The Adolescent Society* (New York: Free Press of Glencoe, Inc., 1961).

FREIDENBERG, EDGAR. *The Vanishing Adolescent* (Boston: The Beacon Press, 1959).

HAVIGHURST, ROBERT J., and BERNICE NEUGARTEN. *Society and Education*, 2d ed. (Boston: Allyn & Bacon, Inc., 1962).

HILGARD, ERNEST R. "A Perspective in the Relationship Between Learning Theory and Educational Practices," in Ernest Hilgard, ed., *Theories of Learning and Instruction*, Sixty-Third Yearbook of National Society for the Study of Education (Chicago: University of Chicago Press, 1960).

REMMERS, HERMANN H. *The American Teen-Ager* (Indianapolis: The Bobbs-Merrill Company, Inc., 1957).

WOODRING, PAUL. "Reform Movements from the Point of View of Psychological Theory," in Ernest Hilgard, ed., *Theories of Learning and Instruction*, Sixty-Third Yearbook of National Society for the Study of Education (Chicago: University of Chicago Press, 1960).

[15] Eric Berne, *Games People Play, The Psychology of Human Relationships* (New York: Grove Press, Inc., 1964), p. 178, *et seq.*

# chapter SEVEN

# The Instructor

*And still they gazed and still the wonder grew*
*That one small head could carry all he knew*—GOLDSMITH.

This phrase from "The Village School Master" neatly sums up the position of the teacher in modern education. In one small head, he has to carry all the knowledge of psychologies about the kids, of the subject that he is going to be teaching them, of the operation of the society for which they are being prepared, and many more. Really, in perhaps an overstatement of the fact, the position of the teacher in the system of instruction is that of a juggler trying to keep all sorts of things in the air in a pattern of order. Instruction takes place within this system and instruction takes place as dialog.

## POSITION OF THE INSTRUCTOR IN THE SYSTEM

**The Dialog Between Wisdom and Innocence.** Generally speaking, the position of the teacher in this system is as the exemplar of wisdom.[1] The phrase "generally speaking" is used because quite often in the modern world teachers find that their innocence shows in many areas and the students' wisdom shows in many areas. So the dialog becomes reciprocal, an interchange among individuals as they search for the image that has been placed in the system.

**The Instructor's Power in the System of Instruction.** The system is dead until some power is put into it. There is the input power of the

---

[1] In this connection it seems worthwhile to point out the traditional academic ranks in higher education in America. The newest and youngest, as instructors, presumably instruct. Then as they move toward wisdom, they, as assistant and associate professors, profess until they reach an eminence wherein they, as full professors, profess fully.

student as he reaches out toward the search image that is his motivation. There is not only a motivation in the psychological sense (an internal drive) but also an idea of propulsion that is sociological. These motivations are the sources of his drive: his peer culture, the teacher, society in general, from within himself.

The teacher also has a power in this system of instruction and it must be examined as one of the parts if the whole is to be understood. His position has an amazing amount of power as he deals with instruction. Power, in any situation, resides in the possession and use of a commodity. In politics the commodity of power is power over people, power over decisions, and power over the directions in which societies will go. In business, the commodity of power is the economic power of what money can do and the power to direct economic choice. In the military field, the power lies in the physical assertion of one group over another, almost a police power. In law, the commodity of power is a social power—the whole system of law bringing its power to bear in one person over another. Often lawyers in a trial, each advocating an opposite side, will be arguing with each other, rather vigorously condemning the other man, his tactics and backgrounds, parental and otherwise. The contest becomes rather emotional with a high degree of conflict, but it is a conflict over law or interpretation of law. At the end of the session, or at the recess, the two lawyers can go out arm in arm and have lunch together and compare notes on how they went at this conflict of power.

It is the same in politics. One of the interesting things about American politics is that the Senate Minority Leader can jump up and down vigorously about the way the administration is carrying on and then five minutes after the Senate has recessed, climb on a plane with the President and go with him for a weekend at his private estate. They are more in a conflict for power than in a conflict of one person against another.

In teaching, the commodity is ideas. Knowledge, in the form of ideas, becomes the means to power but, because schools are often withdrawn from society, these ideas are not often put to a pragmatic test. Therefore, there are often long contests with no decisions. Because it is difficult to render decisions of an absolute nature in the realm of ideas (someone has to win the case in law, the election in politics) the proceedings often become a conflict of personalities. This conflict then takes precedence over the necessary conciliation that goes with instruction. The instructor can present to the learner a certain proposition that he cannot quite accept. The student then, instead of arguing against the proposition, arguing against the idea, begins to argue against the teacher as a person. So the classroom, instead of becoming a forum for the interchange of ideas, turns into a place where there is a conflict of teacher and pupil, where there is quite an argument between personalities. Then each person pulls back a little further into his own idea and retreats to the simplest definition of his own idea. What results is a conflict rather than a reconciliation of points of view.

It is a rather intriguing thing to watch happen and in a very interesting sense a helpful hint to happy teaching because, in presenting the ideas as a search image in the system, the instructor becomes the surrogate of that idea. He is the symbol and the embodiment of that idea. One of the handiest mental attitudes for the instructor to adopt at this particular time is to remember that the learner is not resisting the teacher, he is resisting an idea that the instructor has proposed. However, if the instructor holds an idea that is a very strong one, that has become a part of his own personality, then the learner is resisting the person and a personal adverse confrontation occurs, and the situation becomes one of conflict, not conciliation. This is one of the definitions of power in the instructor's position.

Another area of power that it would be well to examine is the fact that it is the instructor who has the power of choosing the next search image for examination. He is the one who puts into the system the search images. He has the fundamental right, duty, obligation to define the search images and to ensure that they are in the system. He is the one who points out the direction within a search image (the infrastructure), and he also directs the building of search image upon search image to make a larger structure (suprastructure).

In plain, everyday terms, he is the one who tells the kid whether it is a pertinent point or a nonpertinent point, the one who gives the direction of this pursuit of knowledge and the pursuit of search images. He is the one who calls the shots. This is not to say that the learner has no right to place search images in the system. Indeed, he does have the right, and any good instructor will encourage it. But the fact remains that the instructor is the final arbiter as to whether the search image so entered is pertinent, usable, of worth, and to be pursued.

Again, this is a very strong power. It can be an abused power because quite often he will choose as the next search image or within the pattern of one search image a path that is not going to bring about any learning to the students. Maybe they are not interested in it. Maybe they don't have enough background to totally absorb it. Maybe he started off on the wrong level. This is where the power demands a responsibility. One of the facts of life seems to be that for every freedom or power that is granted there is also a concomitant responsibility. The power of choice has the concomitant responsibility for choosing that knowledge that can be learned.

Another type of power of the instructor lies in the input into the system—what he puts into the system to make it move once he has chosen the search image. This power is the power to evoke an image. This is the power to so delineate and define the search image that it can be seen by everyone. What he does is to put an attraction to it by trying to define it, trying to show it up for what it really is so that there can be a mutual examination in the dialog. Jacques Barzun,[2] in a chapter entitled, "Two Minds, One Thought," described this very well:

> How then do you pour a little bit of what you feel and think and know into another's mind? In the act of teaching it is done by raising the ghost of an object, idea, or fact, and holding it in full view of the class, turning it this way and that, describing it—demonstrating it like a new car or a vacuum cleaner. The public has an excellent name for this: "making the subject come to life." The student must see the point, must re-create Lincoln, must feel like Wordsworth at Tintern Abbey, must visualize the pressure of the atmosphere on a column of mercury. The "subject" should become an "object" present before the class, halfway between them and the teacher, concrete, convincing, unforgettable. This is why teachers tend so naturally to use physical devices—maps, charts, diagrams. They write words on the board, they gesture, admonish, and orate. Hence the fatigue and hence the rule which I heard a Dean enunciate, that good teaching is a matter of basal metabolism.

This evoking of an image can take three different patterns.[3] One of them is what Bruner calls "vicarious experience." The teacher establishes the image in such a way that the students can experience in an indirect or perhaps secondhand way. A vicarious experience is one that has a very close analogy to reality but it is not reality itself. A vicarious experience is not necessarily a bad experience, but people would rather have cancer vicariously than actually. Most of us would rather have the experience of fighting in the Civil War vicariously than actually. Most people have enough imagination so that they can fight the Civil War vicariously if given a proper vicarious experience. In a very real sense, school is just a whole series of vicarious experiences. Experience is the best teacher, runs an old saying, but a real experience isn't practical for every learning so vicarious experience meets the need. These experiences are designed to take a student's mind to a different time or to a different place, the time and place of the search image. If, for example, the search image is the concept of the horror of the Civil War as war, a selection from Bruce Catton's *A Stillness at Appomattox* will, vicariously, take the student's mind to that time and that place and provide an emotional set within which the cognitive restructuring of the idea can take place. And, because of the power of that experience, vicarious though it may be, it will probably be such that the learning will be much better than without it.

In our modern technology we have developed a tremendous number of vicarious experiences. We put them on film and call them movies.

---

[2] Jacques Barzun, *Teacher in America* (Boston: Little, Brown, and Company, 1946), p. 31.

[3] Jerome Bruner, *The Process of Education* (Cambridge, Mass.: Harvard University Press, 1962), Chapter 5.

If the search image is such that this vicarious experience cannot operate, there is another experience that Bruner calls the "dramatizing experience." The inherent drama within the subject is shown through a dramatizing experience that brings an image to the learner's attention by playing on the imagination. A student can hear the words that "steam has a power" and he can write it down in his notes and he will remember that steam has power. But when the instructor fills a test tube half full of water, corks it tightly and places it over a Bunsen burner, the learner sees the tube explode and parts of glass go everywhere. Then he gets the sense of the drama of that phrase that steam has power.

Activities can vary from role playing through play reading to a vivid recreation by the instructor of this quality. To give illustration to this substance, to dramatize this point, consider the following:

> The moral dilemma of the Senator from Kansas during the impeachment of President Andrew Johnson illuminates not only that period of history but also one of the deep problems of a representative government —does a representative follow the wishes of his constituents or of his conscience?
>
> Cotton Mather's letter to England concerning the pending arrival of William Penn signed: "Yours in the Bowels of Christ" vividly dramatizes the Puritan doctrine of the elect.
>
> And Adlai Stevenson's comparison of his oratory with President Kennedy's: "When Cicero finished an oration, the people would say, 'How well he spoke.' Ah, but when Demosthenes finished speaking, the people would say, 'Let us march!' " (This is also a dramatic lesson in *charisma* that is necessary for any member of a body politic to know.)

An inventive teacher is not limited to real sources for these activities. An imaginative instructor can pack quite a measure of power into some contrived or simulated material.[4] A word to the conscientious teacher: the fact that the situation is simulated by the instructor does not make it an immoral teaching act. Immorality could lie in trying to pass it off as real, however.

Another way of evoking images is by modeling. Graphs, charts, maps, laboratory apparatus, equations, diagrams are all, in their way, models.

Instructors look to models as ways of establishing a portrait of the structure for the learner. This should become almost automatic in the system of instruction as the instructor seeks to inform the structure in the learning mind. Words become symbols for models but often they are too abstract, or too cumbersome, so the instructor looks to other patterns to construct models.

In a very real sense, the staff and notes on the musicians' racks are the

---

[4] For a thorough examination of the use of simulation in teaching, see Harold Guetzkow, *et al.*, *Simulation in International Relations* (Englewood Cliffs, N.J.: Prentice-Hall, Inc., 1963).

model of the music, flow charts are models of economists' thought, and this book describes a model for instruction.

There are some dangers to the system of instruction in these power inputs by the instructor. In evoking the image, the instructor often shifts the balance between the substance that he is trying to teach and the illustration that he is using to teach it. There is quite a neat balance that a teacher always has to maintain between the substance that he is teaching and the illustration for what he is teaching. Herein lies the danger: if a teacher emphasizes the illustration at the expense of the substance he too often can become, not a teacher, but an entertainer. He becomes a little too flowery. He begins to look for the attractive fact. He begins to teach about the Civil War but distorts a lot of the actual facts of the Civil War by trying to find the color. So the learner has the idea of the Civil War with the bugles sounding in his mind and the drums beating in his mind and the sense of the blood that was on the ground at Gettysburg, but not really with the full total sense of the Civil War. There is a seductive quality about all this business of making the subject very real for the students. The teacher, in his search for reality, can get carried away and look only for the colorful things. Schools have teachers who are very popular because the students find a quality of entertainment about them and at the end of the hour they come out feeling very cheered. Their emotions have been quickened. The adrenalin has begun to flow. But at the end of sober reflection they look back and they say, "What have I learned?" And they really wonder what it is that they have actually been introduced to that is new. Sometimes the feeling is a very gratifying feeling. "I wasn't introduced to anything new but the reintroduction to the old was very charming and I enjoyed every minute of it." And that, in itself, can be a very happy experience for learners, but it is not teaching. This siren call of too much illustration has to be resisted just as much as the other side of heeding the dogmatic call for too much substance.

No teacher wants to be a dry, dusty bore; so many work hard at being colorful. There is another Siren's call when for the first time the students laugh at the teacher or with him. (There is a distinction.) This becomes a very heady experience for the neophyte. Somebody is finally paying attention to him. He has been one man in a mass of students walking along in a big mill called a multiuniversity where nobody seems to care for anything more than his number and bursar's receipt. Then he meets a class, says something fairly funny, and the kids knock themselves out; the heady wine hits. Somebody is paying attention. He has to resist very hard the temptation to run home and buy a copy of "Joe Miller's Joke Book" and start hamming it up in the class. There is a truism in teaching that every teacher has an obligation to be a ham but, like most truisms, and ham, that has to be taken with a lot of salt.

Another sense in which a teacher has a degree of power lies in the fact that he becomes a model to the students. The power derives from the fact that the learner has a drive to search for a model. This is not only in the cognitive sense of search images of ideas, not only in the affective sense of search ideals, but also in the behavior sense. The teacher stands in front as the model of adulthood. All of adult society is wrapped in him for the moment. One of the more interesting times for teachers is when some of their own personal peculiarities as an individual get picked up by the students and they begin to behave like the instructor. They model their behavior after his behavior. A most poignant insight into the search for these models is given by Mrs. John F. Kennedy, "For Jack, history was full of heroes. And if it made him this way—if it made him see the heroes—maybe other little boys will see. . . ."[5]

This idea of modeling accounts for a time in American educational history when the teacher's contracts were written in such a way that the teacher was frozen into a model of the type that the people wanted. Contracts that teachers signed in the 1930s often included agreements to teach a certain number of courses, to spend three weekends out of four in the local community, to teach Sunday School of their choice (as long as it was Protestant). Further they agreed not to smoke, not to drink, not to use profane language, not to fall in love, not to marry during the time of that contract. This was done to insure that the teacher should be a model of the very best for the students.

World War II may not have had many salutory effects, but one of them was the fact that it broke down this pattern, because it created a teacher shortage, and society found that teachers could be effective and also be a little more human than these paragons of virtue that were frozen into molds by these contracts.

Whether or not the instructor is a paragon of virtue or a paragon of vice, there is power derived from being a model.

There is another power rather closely akin to this: the power that comes from being a surrogate of society. The students have a drive toward being members of society and in class the instructor is that society. There is a power inherent in this position and also a threat to the instructor if the society he represents is not totally the society of the student. There is a truism about the teaching profession that the public school teacher in America is a member of the American middle class. Quite often he has gone into public school teaching as a means of movement from the lower class to the middle class. How does that effect the classroom? The teacher goes into the classroom with a middle class value system. Many of his students are not of that particular value system, and the teacher immediately

[5] Quoted by Theodore H. White in *John F. Kennedy Memorial*, New York: *Life* (1963).

senses a chasm between himself and the students. One of the ways this chasm can make itself felt is that the teacher, as a member of the American middle class, feels that everyone else wants to be middle class. Thus, when a young teacher says, "Now if you listen to me and follow me, you, too, can be good, and I will define good as being middle class," the student resists. He says, "I don't want to be middle class. I want to be lower class." And the teacher thinks there is something wrong with the student because he wants to remain lower class. This will have a very interesting impact on the teacher, who will say, "That kid doesn't want to be any good because he doesn't want to be like me." Another illustration of what is meant by this cultural chasm is a sociologist's diagram showing how some concepts are seen in middle-class and in lower-class terms (Table 7–1).[6]

### TABLE 7–1
### THE CULTURAL CHASM

| *The concept of . . .* | *in middle-class terms stands for . . .* | *but to the low class is . . .* |
| --- | --- | --- |
| Authority (courts, police, school principal) | Security—to be taken for granted, wooed | Something hated, to be avoided |
| Education | The road to better things for one's children and oneself | An obstacle course to be surmounted until the children can go to work |
| Joining a church | A step necessary for social acceptance | An emotional release |
| Ideal goal | Money, property, to be accepted by the successful | "Coolness"; to "make out" without attracting attention of the authorities |
| Society | The pattern one conforms to in the interests of security and being "popular" | "The Man"—an enemy to be resisted and suspected |
| Delinquency | An evil originating outside the middleclass home | One of life's inevitable events, to be ignored unless the police get into the act |
| The future | A rosy horizon | Nonexistent. So live each moment fully |
| "The street" | A path for the auto | A meeting place, an escape from a crowded home |

[6] Ralph Segalman adapted this chart from an article presented at the Rocky Mountain Social Sciences Association, Spring, 1965. Reprinted from *Harper's* Magazine (October, 1965), p. 58.

| Liquor | Sociability, cocktail parties | A means to welcome oblivion |
| Violence | The last resort of authorities for protecting the law abiding | A tool for living and getting on |
| Sex | An adventure and a binding force for the family—creating problems of birth control | One of life's few free pleasures |
| Money | A resource to be cautiously spent and saved for the future | Something to be used now before it disappears |

## A NECESSARY BALANCING OF FORCES

There is more to the position of the instructor in the system than power. The important thing is the use of the power rather than the power itself. Use of the power demands a balancing act that has to take into account many forces. This is rather an Aristotelian concept that demands center positions as golden means between extremes in many different areas.

**Cognitive-Affective Balance.** Barzun[7] speaks of this division saying,

> The advantage of "teaching" is that in using it you must recognize— if you are in your sober senses—that practical limits exist. You know by instinct that it is impossible to "teach" democracy, or citizenship or a happy married life. I do not say that these virtues and benefits are not somehow connected with good teaching. They are, but they occur as by-products. They come, not from a course, but from a teacher; not from a curriculum, but from a human soul.

His point is well taken; there must be a balance between the instructor as a technician operating in the cognitive domain and as a warm human working with another human in the affective domain.

**Individual-Group Balance.** Another balance must be made between the individual and the group. A class of 40 students is exactly that—40 individuals. But also, it is one group and the instructor constantly must move back and forth between attentiveness to one person within the group and the total group itself. For a full understanding of this concept, an idea given by Fritz Redl is helpful.[8] As an example of this, Redl gives the following instance:

> Johnny's clowning must be curtailed, or the group goals are too seriously hampered. However, now comes the question of *how* to change Johnny's behavior so that what we do is also harmless to Johnny.

[7] Jacques Barzun, *op. cit.*, p. 9.
[8] Fritz Redl and George V. Sheviakov, *Discipline* (Washington, D.C.: Association for Supervision and Curriculum Development, National Education Association, 1963), p. 26.

Under ideal circumstances the teacher may plan to solve the group problem and Johnny's problem all in one big swoop. This the teacher might do, for instance, by really using a lot of time on Johnny, fixing up his home problem, finding him a nice boys' club where he can do all the clowning he needs without upsetting other people, having him psychoanalyzed, or by meeting whatever his special need may be. However, rarely are the circumstances as ideal as this. Often the teacher does not have this choice, cannot use as much time on changing Johnny's behavior and yet must get results somehow.

What our law of marginal antisepsis demands is that the teacher act at least in such a way that Johnny is not damaged. For instance, just punishing Johnny severely each time he clowns, or expelling him from school, would solve the group problem easily. But what would it do to Johnny, who now is not only without social approval but also more confused than before? Shaming him before the others might also do the trick as far as classroom behavior is concerned. But will this not take away what little social adjustment he has made and drive him into bigger and worse bravado before less sympathetic groups?

The cooperation of other youngsters in the classroom in helping Johnny understand the limits to which he can go will do the trick of checking Johnny's clowning, without making his own adjustment problem more difficult.

The instructor must, of course, remember the old shibboleth of schools—DISCIPLINE. But it is more than a shibboleth. In its proper context it is a learner's life. So it must be regarded as a serious matter. It is impossible to give a recipe for instructor behavior about discipline but some broad statements can help each instructor in shaping his lonely decision as he faces situations in his classes.

One of the best statements of ends for which the instructor must supply the means is by Sheviakov:[9]

> 1. We want discipline which recognizes the *inherent dignity and rights* of every human being, rather than discipline attained through humiliation of the undisciplined.
>
> 2. We want discipline based on *devotion to humanitarian principles and ideals.* In a democratic society, loyalty to the principles of freedom, justice and equality for all rather than discipline based on a narrower, more egotistic affiliation of "*my* group" is essential.
>
> 3. We want *self-direction, self-discipline,* rather than discipline based upon unquestioning obedience to a leader.
>
> 4. We want discipline based on *understanding* of the goal in view rather than discipline based on taking someone else's word for specific appropriate behaviors.[9]

**Learning v. Managing Activities.** Many studies of teachers' activities have shown that much of a teacher's time is given over to just plain managing a classroom. "Get out your pencils," "sit down and shut up," "buy the school annual," "listen to the principal who is about to speak," "do this,

[9] *Ibid.*, pp. 7–8.

do that, do the other thing," become a contrapuntal theme to the melody line of the instructional system. This can reach ridiculous heights; in one 40-minute class the door opened 32 times, with students coming in and out looking for books, messengers coming in and out from the office looking for people. Obviously, classes need managing; obviously, classes are for instruction. Obviously, the instructor must find a balance between these extremes.

**Search Image Balance.** A rather more subtle balance lies between the search image of an idea and the search image of the total system of instruction. This means being attentive to two search images simultaneously —the search image of the idea and the search image of the system. This is where the feedback mechanism comes in. It is through feedback that the instructor senses the degree of structure growing in the learner's mind and, through feedback, he can then feed new information into the system of instruction to correct and add to that structure.

**Suprastructure and Infrastructure Balance.** Of course, there is a balance between working within a search image—the infrastructures—and working on the connection between those images—the suprastructures. This means that the instructor has his mind on the present and on what is going to be happening five minutes hence and five days hence and five years hence. That's enough to drive anybody a little strange.

**Product-Process Balance.** Constantly the instructor must adjust to the interplay between the objectives of teaching for a product and of teaching for a process. Teaching for one can well minimize the other. Thus the teacher must make a conscious effort to move from one realm to the other so that both ends may be served.

**Adult-Adolescent Balance.** A more personal, rather than mental, balance that must be kept in mind is in the social realm—the role of the teacher as an adult in a primarily adolescent society. It is a difficult position for a teacher because it results in a sense of loneliness. That is a hard thing to accept. There is often a sense of panic as if somebody had opened up the cage and sent you in with the tigers. There is another side to this loneliness, overly stated: Consider what happens if there is an absolutely wonderful job of teaching. Who is there to see it?

**Instructor-Entertainer Balance.** A final balance must be struck between being an entertainer and being an instructor. It seems to be a fundamental idea that a teacher has an obligation to be a bit of a ham, that he does have an obligation to bring things alive, that he does have an obligation to be an entertainer to a degree, but there is a balance point there between being an entertainer, between using the flowery examples and actually getting at the instruction that he is supposed to get at. When there is an amount of hamminess, the difference between adult society and adolescent society enters in. What is funny to an adult is not necessarily funny to an adolescent and an attempt to adopt the adolescent sense of humor often results in a dismal failure. The adolescent sense of humor is not always subtle. Too often classrooms are the scene of a rather pitiful exhibition of a teacher being laughed *at* rather than *with*. Not only has he lost his sense of balance but also a sense of integrity.

## INHERENT DANGERS IN THE SYSTEM

It seems to be only fair at this juncture to speak of some thin spots in the ice. There are dangerous areas in this as in most areas of human endeavor. There seem to be about four of them that can be isolated.

**Arrogance.** One of the first is the danger of arrogance. Because of being a model, because of being a surrogate of society, because of searching for power in ideas, there is a danger of becoming rather arrogant, of becoming a bit of a prima donna and saying, "I shall not be challenged," "I have the message," "I am Señor El Magnifico," and "It would be very nice if you were to bow down in my presence and accept the word from on high." (This has a certain messianic quality to it.) Sometimes this arrogance becomes a protective mechanism, and then arrogance often substitutes for ability. Quite often the school-age mind and personality is able to puncture this arrogance rather fast. But then this often makes the armor a little thicker so that the teacher becomes even more arrogant. Then the students become even more puncturing, and then the class becomes nothing more than the throwing of these spears and the holding of this shield.

**The Nonrewards of Teaching.** A more subtle danger takes some time before it asserts itself. This is the danger of what can be called the "nonrewards of teaching." This, perhaps, could be phrased better but it is a feeling that springs from the phenomenon that teaching is done best when the student does not realize he is being taught. The mark of a good teacher lies in the accomplishments of his students. A student may say, "Boy, I learned an awful lot in that course, but it wasn't because of the teacher." Or what hurts, even more, is to have a student, two weeks after an idea has been enunciated, come up with that same idea as if it were absolutely his own idea. The instructor has to sit back very quietly and say, "I know," and resist the temptation of saying, "I told you so." They don't want to be told so. They want to be told that it was their own idea. An architect finishes a building, stands back, looks at it and says, "Aha, this is my building." A musician, a composer, has the same feeling. A teacher finishes his work and stands back to hear the student say, "Aha, this is my own work," little realizing how much of it was what the teacher did. It is a reward, but not a direct one.

**The Disquieting Effect of Instruction on the Learner.** There is another danger that in its way is also an unsettling experience. This is the fact that, by its nature, the instruction process has an initially disquieting effect on the learner. Whenever confronted with a task, the learner goes into this state of anxiety. This anxiety has a disquieting effect on the teacher because he does not like to upset people, generally speaking. Nobody wants to make people unhappy. And he thinks he isn't doing a good job as a teacher because he comes in and says, "Here is the assignment, here is the task, here is the thing to do, here is the search image," and the learner flies into a state of anxiety and says, "What do I do? Where do I go? I don't like this. I don't think this is right! I rebel." That seems to be in the system, but yet it makes the teacher unsettled because he sees this anxiety. He is forced into this role, a little bit, of being the anxiety-arouser, of being a devil's advocate, of being a gadfly in his dialog. So quite often he will get a sense of feedback from the student which means that the student isn't particularly appreciating him as a person. He isn't a nice guy; he isn't a good guy. The "good guy" would just give an "A" and let his students alone. However, the instructor should capitalize on this anxiety for it is the strongest of intrinsic motivations.

**Attachment to the Learner.** A last danger is not so much a danger as it is a pitfall. It is not to be avoided particularly; but there should be a warning. Often, in working with learners through this dialog, a sense of attachment begins to grow. The dialog becomes a thread and the thread winds itself around other threads and becomes a rope, almost a chain, that binds the instructor and learner in a sentimental sort of an attachment.

The dialog in education has been nicely described by Martin Buber.[10] He terms this dialogical relation as "a relation that is characterized in more or less degree by the element of inclusion." Inclusion has its element of communion, and Buber describes the power of the instinct for communion:

> The child lying with half-closed eyes, waiting with tense soul for its mother to speak to it—the mystery of its will is not directed towards enjoying (or dominating) a person, or towards doing something of its own accord; but towards experiencing communion in face of the lonely night, which spreads beyond the window and threatens to invade.

This search for companionship in the community of the dialog can and does readily become the basis for a relationship between instructor and student that is rather sentimental. This is sentimental in more than the Mr. Chips sense although it is that, too. There is a sense of a shared feeling from having striven together in the same system, worked toward the same goals, suffered together in defeat, and rejoiced together in triumphs. When these feelings build on a foundation of a quest for communion and this in an adolescent atmosphere, a genuine attachment can be aroused.

[10] Martin Buber, *Between Man and Man* (New York: The Macmillan Company, 1965), p. 88.

Again, this is not to be decried; genuine human friendship has its sense of glory, of course. The ice gets thin, though, when the teacher must pay for such ecstasy as there is in this with such agonies as there might be in the inevitable parting. Often, a teacher, in the human need for companionship, trades on this atmosphere for attachment and uses it, forgetting that people who use people are the loneliest people in the world.

But, perhaps, the case is overstated. Also in the instructor-learner relation is a little of the Galatea-Pygmalion relation. Here we must accept the authority of Shaw. The last lines of the suffixed essay to his *Pygmalion* warn us that "Galatea never does quite like Pygmalion: his relation to her is too godlike to be altogether agreeable."

## AN AFFIRMATION

Beyond the power, beyond the balances, beyond the danger spots there is the conclusion that somehow or other it does all matter. Through the instruction system, the instructor as well as the learner, sets his eye on broader horizons and has a feeling for a larger destiny for mankind.

This almost visionary quality makes its demands upon the instructor and calls for a sense of humility—"humility to make the foolish wiser and evoke the wisdom of the taciturn," as Justice Frankfurter said of the philosopher and teacher, Alfred North Whitehead.

And because this sense of destiny and the necessary humility can often become burdens as well as glories, it might be well to remember another facet of Whitehead described by Frankfurter: the humor to light up dark places. John F. Kennedy brought this all together very neatly when he wrote:

> There are three things in life that are real:
>     God, human folly and laughter.
> The first two are beyond comprehension
>     So we must do what we can with the third.[11]

There is some of each in teaching. May the proportion you find be pleasing.

## SUGGESTED READINGS

CHARTERS, W. W., JR., "The Social Background of Teaching," in N. L. Gage, ed., *Handbook of Research on Teaching* of the American Educational Research Association (Chicago: Rand McNally & Company, 1963).

HAVIGHURST, ROBERT J., and BERNICE L. NEUGARTEN. *Society and Education,* 2d ed. (Boston: Allyn & Bacon, Inc., 1962), Part 5.

[11] Quoted by Thomas Wicker, *Kennedy Without Tears: The Man Beneath the Myth* (New York: William Morrow & Company, Inc., 1964).

KAUFMAN, BEL. *Up the Down Staircase* (Englewood Cliffs, N.J.: Prentice-Hall, Inc., 1964).

LIEBERMAN, MYRON. *Education as a Profession* (Englewood Cliffs, N.J.: Prentice-Hall, Inc., 1956).

UPDIKE, JOHN. *The Centaur* (New York: Alfred A. Knopf, Inc., 1963).

# VARIATIONS ON
# THE THEME

# chapter EIGHT

# The Ordering of Knowledge

*"Contrarywise," continued Tweedledee, "if it was so, it might be; and if it were so, it would be; but as it isn't it ain't. That's logic."*—LEWIS CARROLL.

Any study of the order in which the subject matter should be entered into the system of instruction has to be made in the light of Tweedledee's warning.

Logic is an honored quality in our society, often honored more in the breach than the observance: to honor it is easy, to observe its laws is difficult. It would seem, however, that the process of in-structuring has within it a place for a definite, ordered progress through the knowledge, a progress that has a rational purpose, that is reasoned, that is predictive. For lack of a better term, we can call it "the line of logic."

This logic line is analogous to the melody of a musical composition. Just as the melody line is not the total of the composition, neither is the line of logic the total of the instruction process. But, just as the melody line is the basic thread upon which the composition hangs, so is the logical thought process the basic thread of the dialog.

As the musician enlarges and embroiders upon the melody line, so does the instructor enlarge and embroider upon the logic line. In both cases this line remains constant and coherent.

As the melody line is the internal structure of the composition, the logic line defines the internal structure of the knowledge in the instructional system. As the performer must find the melody line of the music, the instructor must find the logic line of the knowledge.

In considering this problem of the arranging of knowledge, Philip Phenix offers the following as criteria for decisions about the ordering content:

> . . . the planning of the curriculum requires decisions about the ordering of content. With respect to the sequence of studies three factors are of major importance. The first is the previously discussed factor of integrity,

which suggests that every student at every stage of his learning career should receive some instruction in all six of the realms of meaning. In this way continuous progress toward wholeness of meaning may best be assured.

The second factor in sequence is the intrinsic logical order of the various kinds of meaning. Clearly the languages, being essential to expression in all the other fields, need special initial emphasis. On the other hand, the synoptic fields, depending upon a substantial fund of other meanings to be integrated, can most profitably be pursued at a later stage in the learner's career. The descriptive sciences may be entered upon with less prior preparation than can the moral disciplines, which gain significance only with the assumption of real responsibility. The esthetic and synoptic disciplines are intermediate in the degree of experience required for most effective learning. Thus, the logical interrelations of the realms of meaning have some bearing on the optimum sequence of studies.

The third factor in ordering studies is that of human development and maturation. Empirical studies show that the growing person becomes ready for different types of learning at different stages of growth. These levels of preparedness should be taken into account in planning the sequence of instruction.[1]

## THE DESCRIPTION OF THE VARIATION

One of the basic areas for decisions by the instructor is this area of the logic line in the knowledge. Not only must it be in the system but also it must be given in a certain order to have the greatest effect. As the melody line is built note by note, the logic line is built bit of knowledge by bit of knowledge. As one false note can destroy a melody line, one false note can destroy a logic line.

So the instructor's major decision, it would seem, is the ordering of the knowledge for the fullest effect.

This order lies in two areas: the infrastructure and the suprastructure of the search images. There is an inherent order of search images proceeding from one to another each adding to another to form another, and ever-growing search images result. Also, there is an inherent order within a search image which we call an infrastructure of the search image, an order and coherence of the parts that make up the whole within that search image. So, in brief, we deal here with the relations of the whole to the parts and the parts to the whole. This becomes the basis for the ordering of knowledge in the system of instruction, and it is subject to variation by the teacher.

## CHOICES FOR THE INSTRUCTOR IN THE SYSTEM

These variations are made overtly and deliberately as choices by the teacher.

[1] Philip Phenix, *Realms of Meaning* (New York: McGraw-Hill Company, 1964), p. 9.

**Inductive and Deductive Patterns.** Generally speaking, a teacher may proceed through a subject matter in an inductive fashion or in a deductive fashion and perhaps in a fashion taking into account the student's current knowledge and moving him to unknown knowledges. Of late, much has been made of inductive teaching. There has been a great deal of emphasis on the movement from the specific to the general because it not only brings about a product of instruction in the student's mind, but also teaches him concurrently a process by which he can derive his own knowledge. It has the effect of leading the student to make his own conclusion; it has the effect of involving the student's mind. Perhaps the best thing that can be said about this particular approach is that it does bring the student to a sense of discovery, that it does support one of the hypotheses advanced which says that when facts and details are put into a structured pattern they are retained longer and can be retrieved more easily when needed.

Some fruitful research has been done on the arrangement of the dialog to produce the sense of discovery in the learner's mind. One such project analyzed classroom dialogs and the report makes four major points on the idea of discovery.[2]

One, it is interesting to note, is that the process of discovery moves from the stage of hunch and intuition to a stage of rudimentary analysis and finally to the point where knowledge claims are based on concrete documentary evidence. So it can be seen that the process is not particularly ordered.

The second claim that the authors make is that the students, using historical and social science concepts, employ research techniques and methods of analysis that are used in the real world, not only in the artificial world of schools.

A third point that is made is that the teacher behavior in this particular pattern leads to a better psychological climate that enables the students to become increasingly independent and to probe and question more deeply.

Finally, they found that the method of discovery has a highly motivating effect on the students. It brings about an intrinsic motivation; it brings about the natural search for knowledge given in that intrinsic motivation.

However, this process of discovery is not necessarily limited to the inductive approach.

Discovery is a result of either process; in an inductive approach the whole is discovered by putting all the parts together in a logical order, in a deductive approach the parts are logically derived from a whole.

In any event, what stands out is that the major reason for being attentive to the logical, ordered presentation of knowledge is for an essential discovery to take place by the learner. The direction of the dialog is toward discovery.

[2] Byron G. Massialas, "Teaching Through Discovery," *Social Education* (November, 1964).

Perhaps it is well-nigh impossible to separate the two approaches, inductive and deductive. An observant teacher can notice that as he starts out in an inductive process, he is soon moving toward a deductive process. Perhaps the best way of looking at it is to say that there is a channel from specific to general along which a teacher moves in either direction. The key to the process is to be sure to move to completion. Completion is the time when the student discovers the inherent structure of the several parts and the relationship to the whole.

Now the question rises as to which pattern the teacher should follow. There are times when the subject matter fairly demands one approach or the other. For example, a teacher approached her class with the generalization that the 1920s in American history could be called America's retreat to the future. She tried to do this inductively; that is to say she worked with her students in a dialog and isolated the specific characteristics of the 1920s in American life. What they found were the expected things: the roaring twenties, the farm problem, the American isolation, the return to normalcy, and patterns of this particular type. Then she had the students try to draw these together in an inductive fashion to a generalization, and they were hard put to it to come to the generalization that it was a retreat to the future. They were searching around for some sort of definitions and their logical thought process was an imposed process of trying to find out what the teacher wanted rather than to try to find out what the subject matter had within it. (As is too often a characteristic of American schools, the logical thought process of a student has been changed to finding out what teacher wants rather than being a discovery of what the subject has within it.) However, if the teacher had approached this particular subject deductively, and set up the idea that there is a generalization, that the twenties were America's retreat to the future, the search image would have been America's retreat to the future. The first entry would be the definition of that idea, subsequent entries into the system develop the idea, find the parts to support that whole idea, then, when they all come together into the final pattern, the teacher can observe the student discovering how the specifics add up to the total. This would have been a deductive approach logically derived from the type of subject matter.

So, in summary, it would seem that the teacher is working toward a process of inquiry in his classroom and a process of discovery in his classroom. He has choices to make in the order of the knowledge he is imparting.

## CONSIDERATIONS GOVERNING THE INSTRUCTOR'S CHOICES

What are some of the considerations that are necessary in making these choices? There seem to be two. One of them lies in the realm of communications theory and the other lies in the realm of the verbal medium for the message, or semantics. So let us turn to communications theory. Before we can penetrate deeply into this we must remember that communications theory and teaching theory are not the same and that communications theory has contributed to bright and sparkling vocabulary to the work of the people in the theory of instruction. So, using this vocabulary, we can examine some of the patterns of communication and find the analogies to teaching situations.

**Communications Patterns and the System of Instruction.** Claude Shannon, one of the pioneer workers in the field of communication, has a diagram of the communications process in which he speaks of an information source, a message, a transmitter, a signal, a channel, a receiver, and a destination (see Fig. 8–1).

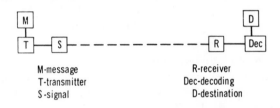

M-message         R-receiver
T-transmitter     Dec-decoding
S-signal          D-destination

FIG. 8-1.

Also there is in this communication system a concept that he calls "noise." Noise is the quality that acts on the signal to vary it in unexpected ways.[3] Noise can be physical noise such as the rumble of a machine or the sudden dropping of a book or a sneeze, something of that nature, or it can be something else in the physical realm in the way of poor light, in the way of a cold feeling, of a cold draft, something that is sensed by the person in such a way that it varies the signal that is being sent to him. Also, noise can be, in a nonphysical sense, in the patterns of communication.

The information source selects the desired message out of a set of possible messages. The transmitter changes the message into the signal, which is sent over a selected communications channel. A receiver accepts the message and decodes it back into the message and delivers it to the destination. The noise which varies this particular signal can be overcome in several ways so that the system can operate. One way is through redundancy. The English language is about one-half redundant. This sentence can be both a thought and an example of that truth. For instance, we can reduce this redundancy by crossing out the "the," "language," "about," and there remains the same thought, "English is half-redundant." Then, to reduce the re-

---

[3] Chapter 10 uses some of this vocabulary and shows how "noise" affects the instructional system. For a graphic presentation of these ideas see the film *A Communications Primer,* by Charles Eames. Its influence is acknowledged.

dundancy more, we can even cross out the "is" and have "English half-redundant."

This illustrates the fact that we have built into our own language-system patterns of repetition and redundancy that will act to overcome noise. In other words, if you didn't get the message in the first word, you got it in the second word, if you didn't get the information in the first part of the message, you got the information in succeeding parts of the message.

A second way of overcoming noise is to aim the beam of the channel. Taking a more precise aim on the destination eliminates noise. This is obvious to a teacher. If little Willie is sitting in the back of the room near the window and looks out over the new construction of a new school wing and has a hard time hearing because of the operating shovels, the teacher can go back to the corner of the room and speak closer to Willie, thereby aiming the beam of the signal, so that Willie finds that noise in the system is overcome. This rather careful beaming of the signal is necessary, of course, for this communications pattern to operate.

A third way that we can overcome noise is by increasing the power of the transmission. Increasing the power of the transmission can be accomplished on several levels. The simplest level is to increase the physical power of transmission. Now when little Willie is unable to hear in the back of the room because of the noise from outside, the teacher shouts, overcoming the noise, his voice level is at a higher pitch than the noise outside, so Willie hears. It's as simple as that.

The transmission of the message has an emotional power. The emotional power can be increased positively by putting some sugar on the message, such as saying, "Willie, you are a good little boy and you can hear and I like you very much and so you can hear what I am about to say." Or we can increase the emotional power in a negative sense, saying, "Willie, if you don't hear what I say, you're liable to fail the course."

A final way of overcoming noise as it enters into the communications system is to duplicate the message by another signal. This is done constantly in the classroom when a student reads the book and then the teacher repeats the same content that is in the book by the use of another signal. The signal in the book was the written word, the signal of the teacher is the spoken word. Quite often they are completely different words but they are a duplication of the same message by another signal. Now, if Willie cannot be reached because there is too much noise outside, the teacher can write a note to Willie on the board, and Willie gets the message through another signal.

How does all this pertain to teaching? In this particular way: the communications system has messages going from source to destination. In the system of instruction the instructor is the source, and the destination is the learner, while the messages are the search images that are sent across the channels. These are broken down into parts that can be small enough to fit across the channel without creating noise and still be received at the destination in such a way that they can be decoded. The instructor must decide which part comes first, which part comes second, which comes third. This decision is based on some kind of order for the presentation of the subject matter. The logic behind this order can be based on the inherent structure of the subject or dictated by patterns of the learning process.

Each of these parts are points of a decision and the selecting and arranging of the parts by the student makes a whole which is a unity. In the terminology that we have used heretofore, the student discovers the unity out of the parts that have been sent to him across this communication channel.

There is a tremendous amount of information that is sent across the channel. Consider the sentence that you are now reading. Look at each of the points of decision. Each of the points of decision in these sentences is a letter. The letters are formed in different ways; the "s" is a squiggle, the "i" is a line, the "o" is a circle, and so on until 26 different forms are made. These letters are put together and become parts of a unity that are called syllables, which in turn become parts of a unity called words, which in turn become parts of a unity called phrases, which in turn become parts of a unity called sentences, which in turn become parts of a unity called paragraphs and add up to a larger and larger message that is being sent across. But in reading this sentence that you are now reading, your mind is decoding each of these parts, selecting and arranging them to make a whole which is unity. So there is a mass of information that can be sent.

Where does communication theory meet with decision theory in teaching? Communications theory deals with the process of sending parts across channels to receivers, who in turn add these parts to become totals. What it means is, of course, that the whole must be broken down into parts in a logical way that can be restructured in the learner's mind in the image that they were started on the other side of the communications pattern. The order and the arrangement of the parts is an overt decision on the part of the teacher. Often this decision is made on an intuitive basis; once in a while the decision is made on a rational basis.

Decision theory deals with making proper choices with reference to the whole by feedback to the whole or model. An analogy of this is the action of a hand reaching down to pick up an object on the table. The hand moves out toward that object and is guided to that object by the mechanism of sight which establishes a model in the mind for the action of the arm to follow. An infinite number of decisions is made by each of the nerve cells guiding muscles there. A number of decisions is made in picking an object from the table of such a magnitude that if they were reduced to the points of decision in a halftone photograph of clarity, there would be enough points to cover the earth several times. This is the magnitude of decision processes in the very simple act of picking up a pencil. Consider, if you can, the amount of decision making that a mind goes through in deciding among the massive choices that it has: the precise words, the precise phrase, the precise sentence, to mirror an image and send it across so that the image can be added to other images, can become parts to other wholes, to become a unity.

**Semantics and Instruction.** Let us turn now to another consideration that the teacher must bear in mind when he makes the decisions as to the order of the subject matter that he is going to teach. These considerations have to do with the content of the message. It is here that we must touch upon the idea of semantics. In this particular sense, we realize that words become the symbols for communication and are sent across the channel to the destination. But because the words are symbols and not reality we find that they can be a noise in the system. One of the first things to accept is the fact that there is a difference between the word and the reality that that word represents. The words are symbols of reality. The symbol "apple" is not an apple. "Apple" is a word. One of the simplest and most effective ways to understand this is to pick up a pencil and in the margin of the book write the word "barn." Then when you look at it, you say, "What is this word?" Perhaps you may say, "What is this?" The answer is obvious. It is graphite on paper. But because we are verbal minded, we immediately think not "What is this object?" but "What is this word?" This word, then, becomes to us in the English language, barn.

But now let us move to a second consideration. Words symbolize reality and so the word "barn" to somebody in the midwest of the United States means a very sturdy structure, probably red, probably with white trimming, probably two-storied with food storage up above and animal storage down below. But also, the word "barn" to somebody in the American southwest where the climate is much less rigorous, can mean nothing more than four posts with a roof that provides shade for the storage of food while the animals roam at will outside. So when one person says "barn," he, being a good midwesterner, is representing and symbolizing that big red building out in the field, abstracting from that reality through the word "barn." And an American from the southwest hearing that word, is listening, sees it in his mind as the reality of the four-posted roof rather than the sturdy red structure. Thus communication doesn't take place because the words abstract from different realities. We have noise in the communication system caused by words and symbols.

Then we enter an even more slippery area in dealing with semantics: words may also abstract from nonreality or from ideas. If they abstract from ideas, the chances for faulty communication increase very, very markedly. Different words may be used to symbolize the same ideas and create a noise in the transmission that impedes the process of communication. Many people have derived comfort from the Twenty-Third Psalm that is written in the Bible in familiar, poetic lines.

> The Lord is my Shepherd, I shall not want;
> He maketh me to lie down in green pastures;
> He leadeth me beside the still waters;
> He restoreth my soul;
> He leadeth me in the paths of righteousness for His name's sake.
> Yea, though I walk through the valley of the shadow of death,
> I will fear no evil: for Thou art with me,
> Thy rod and thy staff they comfort me.
> Thou preparest a table before me in the presence of mine enemies:
> Thou anointest my head with oil; my cup runneth over.

The same idea has been written in another way.

> The Lord is my external-internal integrative mechanism,
> I shall not be deprived of gratification for my viscerogenic hungers or my
>     need-dispositions.
> He motivates me to orient myself towards a non-social object with effec-
>     tive significance,
> He positions me in a non-decisional situation,
> He maximizes my adjustment.
> Although I entertain masochistic and self-destructive id impulses,
> I will maintain contact with reality for my superego is dominant.[4]

The idea is the same: the words are different. One wonders if the comfort derived is the same. The words denote the same idea but there is a connotative glow surrounding them that can change the message markedly to the point that one could be accepted and the other could be rejected.

Another problem with the use of words as a channel of communication lies in the fact that there is only a finite number of words. Because words represent an infinite number of objects, we find that words take on many meanings. Consider a common word "fast." We have the phrase "fast color," which means that the color doesn't run. And yet, we can have a "fast horse" who does run. We can find a ship "fast at the dock" which means that it is not loose. And yet we have a "fast girl" who is loose. And we have the idea of the "fast" with its religious connotations, and we have the idea of a "fast buck" which has connotations something other than religious.

Let us drive this home with one more story: An army company was marching in due order down a road and the sergeant in command, seeing a truck approaching, gave the order, "Bear to the right." To a man, the company took off down the hill to the left. This takes on a little bit more meaning when we add that the company was composed completely of mountain types, to whom "bear" meant a big, black, furry animal. When

---

[4] Robert A. Baker, ed., *A Stress Analysis of a Strapless Evening Gown and Other Essays for a Scientific Age* (Englewood Cliffs, N.J.: Prentice-Hall, Inc., 1963).

somebody said, "Bear to the right," they took off to the left as fast as they possibly could.

Sometimes we find that words are used to protect *against* thoughts. We employ euphemisms constantly to protect us against the reality that words may symbolize. We speak of loved ones passing away, rather than dying. We speak of terminal illness rather than cancer. Many times we employ phrases with a little less emotional loading in order to protect us from the reality behind that does have a very heavy emotional load. ("Stupid" becomes "slow learner".) Again, because of the fact that a euphemism isn't a true representation of reality, we find that words do not always communicate the ideas. Another way in which words protect us against thoughts is that often the communications channel or the system of instruction is filled with symbols that just weave a spell rather than convey any thoughts, and so we find that the communicator deals in a spell of words. They sound very, very good but they really contain nothing.

Finally, words protect us against thoughts in the sense of conditioning. We hear somebody yell, "Fire," and we immediately run, without thinking, because we have been conditioned to flee from the evil of fire. We reach out for something and somebody says, "No!" We stop, without thinking, because by that word, we have been conditioned against reaching. The advertising industry quite often tries to establish patterns in such a way that people are conditioned so that, instead of thinking "cigarette," they think of a particular brand and ask for that particular brand.

Not only do words protect against thoughts but also words influence thoughts. Benjamin Whorf maintained that not only do thoughts shape our language but also our language shapes our thoughts. He points out that a great deal of the thought process of the western world stems from the cause and effect relationship of the Indo-European languages with their subject-predicate arrangement, as distinguished from the ideographic languages of some of the Eastern cultures.

Then there is a final way in which words *arouse* thoughts. Analysis of propaganda techniques reveals methods by which words are used to influence thoughts. Analysis of propaganda techniques have found several different ways in which propaganda arouses thoughts. Words become weapons in human conflict.

**Things That Ain't Logic.** In the ordering of knowledge for teaching, the line of logic of that knowledge provides the structure in the same way that the music staff provides the structure for the composer to keep the notes of melody in order. But the line of logic is not quite so graphically clear as the staff that holds the melody. In that case a way to define the line is to define some of the things that "ain't logic," in the Tweedledeeian sense.

Logic is used by the human mind in its two-fold struggle to attain knowledge (the product) and to handle it (the process). This is a difficult task, and mistakes are constantly being made. These fallacies can be described. For purposes of brevity and clarity we can limit our discussion to a description of those fallacies that creep into thinking rather than those that arise from attempts to create new knowledge.

It is difficult to classify these fallacies positively, but there seems to be two broad types: formal or procedural, and material. Formal fallacies involve some breach of the procedures of logic, whereas the material fallacies result from false assumptions or misapprehensions of the content.

There are some procedural fallacies that crop up in the mental activities of learners (and instructors).

*Hasty generalization.* This is otherwise known, rather loosely, as jumping to a conclusion. It is the making of a general statement on the basis of insufficient specific evidence. It is summed up in the aphorism, "One swallow does not make a spring."

*Overgeneralization and overprecision.* Closely related to the procedure of drawing the general from the specific is the fallacy of being too general and the fallacy at the opposite extreme of being too precise. To say that it is always cold in Pennsylvania rather neglects the summer; to give the listener the total statistics of temperature is burdensome and boring.

*Simple extremes.* This fallacy is rather tempting and dramatic to simpler minds but nonetheless fallacious. This fallacy is characterized by reasoning that reaches to the opposite extreme without attention to middle ground. "If you are not with me, you must be against me," is a common example. It seems to be rather characteristic of adolescent minds, where it is manifested by an adoration of the attractive and hate of the unattractive. At least the words they use would warrant that conclusion.

*Post-hoc reasoning.* Looking for causes after an event is part of the human quest but attribution of the wrong cause constitutes the fallacy. Often this wrong cause is selected in order to make the event more acceptable. A person waking with a pounding headache after a night of revelry could, probably falsely, attribute his ailment to the idea that he had been working too hard.

*Begging the question.* There is a certain circularity in the fallacious reasoning of giving the conclusion as a reason for the conclusion. The old saying among psychologists that "intelligence is that which is measured by what we call intelligence tests" begs the question of defining intelligence.

*Vagueness-over-precision.* In the use of words to communicate thoughts, two fallacies can be committed, both of which err in being wide of the mark of exactness. To be vague communicates too little; to be overprecise may communicate too much by making it difficult to sort out the wheat of worth from the chaff of detail. "Poetry is best when it casts images of the ineluctable in man and in nature. In the redundant, redounding of the two, poetry reflects the constant interplay of modern existence" perhaps means something but it seems to commit the fallacy of vagueness. The error in the other direction would define poetry as a rhymed metric pattern of five, seven, or nine lines and thus constrict poetry by an overprecise definition.

Material fallacies result from a misconstruing of the material of the knowledge.

*Fact v. opinion.* The first fallacy is to base the reasoning on an opinion that is mistaken for a fact. A fact is verifiable; an opinion is an attitude to the fact. A fact: the day's high temperature was 30 degrees. An opinion: the day was cold.

*Nonsequitur.* This fallacy is characterized by drawing a conclusion not supported by the facts under consideration. The beautiful blond sits in the front row, takes notes with vigor, laughs at the instructor's sallies into humor, and generally graces the world with her presence. To say that she is a good student is a *nonsequitur.* Given those facts, it does not follow that she is a good student. (Of course, there could be further argumentation and disputation over the definition of a student.)

*Composition and division.* These fallacies are quite similar to those of errors in generalization but enough different, and often enough committed, to bear further examination. The fallacy of division is the converse: attributing to a part the characteristic of the whole. Using the same girl who graced the class in the previous example, to say that she is intelligent because the class in which she appears is of high intelligence would be a fallacy of division. A fallacy of composition would be to declare the class as being beautiful because she is.

*Ad populum.* An appeal to the popular feeling rather than the constituent parts of the argument makes this fallacy. It has a bandwagon effect that says the reasoning is good because it results in the popular position.

*Ad hominem.* Related to this fallacy is the fallacy of arguing to the man that holds the idea rather than the idea itself. "That book cannot be much because, after all, look at the college the author attended!"

With these ideas on the ordering of knowledge, we can now turn to the next means by which the instructor can vary the system—by deciding on the strategies that will be used in the system.

## SUGGESTED READINGS

DEWEY, JOHN. *How We Think* (Boston: D. C. Heath & Company, 1910).
——. *Logic: The Theory of Inquiry* (New York: Holt, Rinehart & Winston, Inc., 1938).
SANDERS, NORRIS M. *Classroom Questions, What Kinds?* (New York: Harper & Row, Publishers, 1966).

# chapter NINE

# Strategies for Instruction

*. . . for only the understanding heart . . . can comprehend the infinite possibilities of Reality and, being confident, can understand the hearts of other men and speak to them in turn with trust and clarity. . . .*—ROBERT OSBORN.

The word "strategies" for instruction conjures up visions of armies being deployed back and forth across the battlefield with generals plotting means of overcoming other armies, locked in mortal combat. This is a misleading term because education and instruction should not be viewed so much as conflict as conciliation. The quote that is the theme for this chapter is a more appropriate point of view than is the word "strategies." However, because "strategies" has been given a great deal of current use in the field of instruction, we can use the term with the caution that the dictionary definition of strategies deals with conflict where the purpose of education deals more with the conciliation of conflicting ideas, the finding of gray matter between black and white extremes, the mutual search for truth in the dialog. What is needed is a feeling on the part of the instructor of understanding the infinite possibilities of reality, and the hearts of the people in the instructional dialog so that there can be a communication with trust and clarity, a communication that leads to a necessary instruction, rather than a strategy for conflict.

Earlier, in our discussion of the dialog in instruction, reference was made to Martin Buber's ideas of a communion in the dialog. He also adds the ingredient of trust to the dialog, saying:

> I have referred to the child, lying with half-closed eyes, waiting for his mother to speak to him. But many children do not need to wait, for they know that they are unceasingly addressed in a dialogue which never breaks off. In face of the lonely night which threatens to invade, they lie preserved and guarded, invulnerable, clad in the silver mail of trust.[1]

[1] Martin Buber, *Between Man and Man* (New York: The Macmillan Company, 1965), p. 98.

Mystical as it may sound, there is much wisdom in the observation. Any teacher, reflecting an attempt to reach a rebel in class—a person outside the warmth and trust of social acceptance—can testify to the difficulty, if not impossibility, of communication. It is here that conciliation can easily side into conflict.

Of all the variations on the logic line that must be taken into account in the process of instruction, the one that is most able to be regulated by the instructor is the one dealing with his choice of the strategies that he will employ as he, in the dialog, works with the students toward the structuring of the search image in their minds.

## THE DESCRIPTION OF THE VARIATION

In order to define the choice of strategies, let's first look at the teacher's total act in the instructional process. Broudy and Palmer[2] describe the several phases or steps that occur in the teaching act. These phases or steps are in every teacher's strategic behavior. They are in every pattern, regardless of the particular style or mode that the teacher is using. These phases are not listed in serial order; that is to say that they are not listed in the order in which they have to occur; however, there seems to be a kind of general order of occurrence here, but some can occur before others.

**The Phases of Instruction.** The first phase is the "preparation for instruction." This is the period before the instructor meets the pupil, before the instructor-student dialog takes place. Planning is the word that characterizes this preparation phase, when the instructor gathers his materials, makes notes on what he wants to cover, looks at the psychological and sociological background of the group of students whom he will be instructing, and perhaps rehearses the type of behavior that he will employ when the dialog begins. Again, in this particular realm, the strategies govern the different forms of preinstructional preparation.

Little needs to be said to the conscientious teacher about this planning phase. Imagination will show that if you don't know the material well you must do some thorough preplanning and, conversely, if you do know it well you must plan so that an ordered dialog will take place. Also, it doesn't take a very long time for a new teacher to understand the aphorism, "You'll never teach all you know, but you'd better know all you'll teach."

A second phase is the phase that Broudy and Palmer call "motivation." Any theory of instruction must, of course, take into account the idea of motivation in the pupils. Other than to mention the fact that the instruction proceeds best if the motivation is intrinsic, we do not need to repeat what was said there. However, it must be noted that the instructor has to

[2] Harry S. Broudy and John R. Palmer, *Exemplars of Teaching Method* (Chicago: Rand McNally & Company, 1965), p. 8 *et seq.*

give more attention to motivation than to any of the other phases. This is a fairly obvious point and it can be explained with the obvious answer that very often a student's wishes and an instructor's wishes are at variance and the instructor has to find some way of bringing the student to a motivation if the student is to learn his particular subject. This seems to be inherent in the course of events. Instructors, again, have to find a mean between the extremes of giving material to the student that is of interest only to them (in short, entertaining the student with those things that are of interest) or on the other hand, of giving material to the students regardless of its inherent interest for the student. Finding the middle ground in this choice of interesting material versus what we might call necessary material is, again, a decision and a problem for the instructor.

Another phase, and this phase leads directly into the instructional process, is the presentation of the search image to the student. (Broudy and Palmer use the term, "the presentation of the learning task.") This is the entry into the system of instruction of the bit of knowledge that is to be learned, being structured for the student by the instructor and in-structured in the student's mind through his learning acts.

The *art* of teaching, of course, enters into this particular type of presentation. Here the teacher proceeds almost intuitively, basing his steps on the feedback that he gets from the students as 25 to 35 individuals, or as one total class. It is here where the teacher must rely on his sensibility, experience, and genuine common sense in order to proceed with a minimum of disturbance for the system of instruction.

The fourth stage takes place almost concurrently with the third stage. Broudy and Palmer term this "the inducement of a trial response." In our terminology, it means the inducement of some sort of reaction from the student that will come through the feedback mechanism to the teacher. This is the most informal evaluative device that allows the teacher to determine how the student is moving along in his progress toward understanding the total search image. For example, suppose that the search image is a description of San Francisco during the height of the gold-rush period and the teacher has been working toward an understanding of the boom atmosphere, of the crowded conditions, of the hurly-burly, of the number of new people pouring into the city every day on their way to the gold fields. If the teacher gets the student's verbal reaction that the steamships are crowded in the harbor and that the clouds of smoke from the ships hid the sun—then he knows that there is something wrong, mainly because steamships were not sailing into San Francisco harbor until long after the gold-rush period. In this rather crude way we can illustrate what we mean by the inducement of a trial response or correction by a feedback mechanism.

This, of course, leads us into the fifth phase, the correction of the learner's held structure. This, of course, means that the teacher constantly receives a feedback from the student, weighs that feedback in terms of his search image, and then corrects the student or students toward a better perception of what the search image really contains.

Finally, the last step in this actual instructional dialog is the idea of the fixation of the correct search image. Through some process of operation, the teacher must fix in the students' minds the structure so that it will be held, not for the test on Friday, not for the grade in the course, but for an extended future. Somehow it must be given a permanent place in the memory bank, ready for retrieval whenever the student needs to use it. Perhaps one of the best ways to fix this response is to show the students the inherent value and meaning of this search image so that it will become part of their structure of the subject.

The seventh and last stage is the more formal stage of test response and evaluation. The teacher judges the student on the adequacy of his ability to manipulate the material that he has been given through his dialog of instruction. In formal instruction patterns this last phase is separated from the other phases by a considerable time and the student is asked to hold search images in abeyance, bring them together with other search images, weave the ideas together into a greater fabric of knowledge.

These middle steps—numbers three, four, five, and six—are the areas within which occur the dialog of instruction. The teacher enters into that dialog with a search image. He then senses the feedback from the students; then he corrects any distortions or misknowledges that the student might have; then he works toward some way of fixing this in the student's mind, of getting the student to internalize, or work toward the process of internalization of, the subject matter. These are the areas where the strategy decisions are made. It is in these four areas where the teacher can vary his presentation, can vary his strategies, can vary his order so that better learning can take place.

## CHOICES FOR THE INSTRUCTOR

Let us now turn toward an examination of the modes of operation that a teacher can use in this particular realm of presenting the search image; sensing the feedback, correcting the search image in the student's mind, and fixing that search image in his mind.

Many times the instructor's decision is based on the type of material that constitutes the search image. Many times it is based on the type of the student mind that he is dealing with, and many times it is based on his own particular teaching personality. Most often the decisions are based on a combination of these.

Basic to an understanding of these modes of operation for a teacher is the idea mentioned in previous chapters, but mentioned again in this connection for reinforcement, the idea of a necessity for maintaining a balance between substance and illustration. The teacher has the obligation in this particular realm of operations to make sure that the student understands the material by means of apt illustrations, but he must also make sure that the substance is not hidden by the drama and the glory of the illustrations.

**The Expository Mode.** With this basic reservation in mind, let us turn to the first mode of operation, which is the expository mode. In this particular mode of operation, the teacher, as the word connotes, exposes the search image to the learner. He peels back a little of the cover so that the learner can peek in. He opens the door so that the learner can see through to what the structure really is. This expository mode is characterized by certain verbal acts on the part of the teacher.[3] One of these is the act of describing. Describing has four or five different forms, one of which is stating a fact or idea, a mere statement of what it is. Another form is reporting findings on facts and ideas. Another is defining an idea. Another one is designating a particular pattern or categorization. All of these are acts within the describing process that a teacher does in the expository mode. As can be seen, these are acts that are centered in the teacher's mind. They are sent into the system of instruction by the teacher's power input of such drama or vicarious experience as he is able to summon on this particular material. When the teacher is operating in this particular expository mode, using the verbal act of describing, the teacher's voice dominates the classroom, and, in a sense, the teacher is going through his own verbal, oral examination.

A step up from sheer description is the other verbal act that the teacher does in this expository mode. This verbal act can be called *explaining*. This tends to involve the student's mind a little bit more than the mere description of a particular search image. Explaining has in it the verbal acts of classifying, comparing, contrasting. So it is that, with these three verbal acts, the student's mind becomes more involved with the subject. The first describing brings the student more toward a process of memorization or translation than anything else. Explaining patterns in this expository mode may move him up a little bit on the scale toward interpretation and application and hopefully involve his mind more. However, it takes an adroit student mind capable of vicarious thoughts to follow teacher explanations constantly. The student involvement during teacher explanations is based on experiences that the student may have had and is generally a very passive involvement.

**The Examinatory Mode.** This mode of operation by the teacher is designed to involve the learner's mind more than the expository. In this mode of operation the instructor has two choices for operation: one is an examination of a hypothesis, the other of a speculation.

[3] These categories are a rearrangement of ideas expressed in B. O. Smith, "A Study of the Logic of Teaching" (Urbana, Ill.: University of Illinois Press, mimeographed 1963).

This implies an examination of a proposition by both instructor and learner that accents the process of knowledge as much as the product of knowledge.

These propositions can be of two types: hypotheses and speculations. The hypothesis is a proposition proposed by the instructor to which there can be a convergence of the minds of the learners and a commonality, if not a truth, be accepted. A speculation is a proposition that resists conveyance and perhaps invites divergence. On this level the accent in the system of instruction is completely on the process.

Nevertheless, on these levels there is an examination by the instructor and the learner in their joint dialog as they search for the structure within the pattern of the search image. The major verbal act at this particular level is the verbal act of *inferring*. In this act, the teacher establishes certain conditions, and the student learns from them by going through acts of inference. This is not quite correct, in that the teacher also goes through these acts of inference with the student. So here we have the idea we have expressed so often in this book, that of the double-bladed approach to purpose of teaching—the idea of teaching both a product and a process.

Let us look a little more at these patterns of inferring that a teacher can use. The first one is by analogy. Analogy is the employment of a certain metaphoric sense on the part of the teacher wherein he describes something as being like something else. Since the new material is like a material that the student has already experienced, a transfer takes place and hopefully an insight can lead to learning. As an example, we can say that the Brazilian system of government is like the American system of government because (a) Brazil is called the United States of Brazil, (b) there is a series of states in a federal relationship, (c) there is a division of power in the federal government between the judicial, the legislative, and the executive branches. Then the instructor can say to the student that the government of Brazil is analogous to that of the United States and the learner, being conversant with the government of the United States, therefore sees the structure of the government of Brazil by this process of analogy. The process of analogy, then, is to find something within the student's own experience that is quite similar to the new search image and to work from this pattern of the old to the new. This is reasoning by analogy on the learner's part and teaching by analogy on the instructor's part.

There are inherent dangers in this, and they are perhaps summed up very well by Samuel Butler's statement, "Though analogy is often misleading, it is the least misleading thing we have." This means that the use of analogy is never going to be an accurate transmission of the knowledge. However, it will become as accurate as we can get with the tools that we have in communication in this particular realm.

Now we can turn to another area of inference—an area that has been called conditional inference. In this particular teacher verbal behavior, the instructor establishes certain conditions in the student's mind and lets the student draw his own conclusions. In other words, the student infers from some of the conditions. As an example, let us say that a teacher is giving a course in United States history and describes the circumstances of the election of 1876 when Hayes and Tilden were contesting for the presidency of the United States. The knowledges that are under consideration are the conditions of that particular period. Tilden had a greater popular vote than Hayes, but finally Hayes became the president because he gained more electoral votes. The votes came in a meeting of the electoral college and were based on an agreement to end Reconstruction.

These are the conditions. The student may infer from these conditions that the electoral college does not represent the American electorate's wishes during an election. This was not the teacher's object, perhaps, at the time; it could well have been to show the maneuvering that ended Reconstruction as a formal policy.

This conditional inference can take place in a student's mind without the teacher's so desiring. However, there are times when the teacher will establish certain conditions and feel that the student will make the necessary inference from those conditions. This becomes a process that is more laden with student thought than the processes described under the expository mode. This means that the student reaches his own conclusion, the student leaps toward a particular conclusion.

**The "Aha" Phenomenon.** In the examinatory mode of operations that the teacher is employing, there is a certain pattern of intellectual behavior on the part of the student that determines how well the mode is operating. This phenomenon in the student has been called by psychologists the "aha" phenomenon, and it is marked in the students' verbal behavior by such phrases as, "Aha, I've got it," or, as some psychologists call it, the "eureka" phenomenon (I have found it). What happens is that the teacher establishes in the student's mind a certain pattern, probably in the form of a problem. That pattern is followed by the student until he reaches, on his own, an insight—a light goes on in his mind.

As an example let us examine the following problem:

O  T  T  F  F  S  S  __  __  __

The problem here is for the learner to fill in the last three blanks with letters that will carry on the same continuity established in the first "givens." The answer to this is obvious. The blanks should be filled in with the letters "E," "N," and "T." If you have filled them in like that, you have understood that the whole sequence is the first letters of the words for the first ten numbers in our American numbering system. Now that you see it perhaps you feel a sense of "Aha, that's what they were driving at." We hope that as you read through this you get a sense of this "aha" phenomena. "Aha, now I see how this problem is to be solved. Now I see the conditions and what can be inferred from those conditions and the problem is solved."

These ideas of the two modes of instructor verbal behavior and instructor verbal acts can now be entered in the chart elements of the parts of the system (see Fig. 9–1). The teacher verbal acts have the same incremental

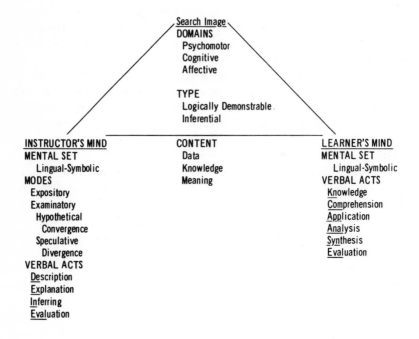

FIG. 9.1 Elements of parts of the system.

pattern that seems to be inherent in the learner verbal act side of the chart. Again, it seems that each of these acts is involved, to a degree, before the final act can take place.

## CONSIDERATIONS GOVERNING INSTRUCTOR'S CHOICES

Now that we have discussed some of these modes of operation open for the teacher and the choices for his behavior pattern in the verbal realm of his teaching, let us turn to some considerations governing his choice of modes of operation.

**The Teaching Personality.** The first of these is the teacher himself in the system. One of the interesting characteristics of this teaching process is that the teacher tends to develop his own teaching personality which often tends to be somewhat different from the personality that expresses itself in the other realms of his life. There has been little research to prove this idea except that every experienced teacher and experienced student notes the fact that the teacher has a little bit of the fire-dog quality in him. When he hears the bell sound, he starts to run. He starts to go to work assuming a different personality in his work. In a subsequent chapter we will take up more thoroughly some of these different teaching personalities. But it is sufficient for our purpose here to point out the fact that quite often the first job of the new teacher is to assess his own teaching personality. He may enter his first classroom convinced that he can best do the job of teaching by being a very formal person working with students' minds in a very calm, exploratory way. Then he may find that he is made very unhappy by a sense of disorganization that results from this approach, and he quickly changes his teaching personality to that of being a fairly ordered teacher whose operations go clicking along from one step to the next. He may feel that he will work with the students in the affective domain, accept them for what they are, try to make them better people. Then he may find, when he starts to teach, that his major interest is not particularly in this psychological area but more in the cognitive area of re-structuring knowledge in the students' minds. He may find that his personality changes in a classroom from what he thought it was going to be. This is not to be decried; this is a perfectly normal pattern of development and the best thing that could be said about it is that every teacher should recognize this and recognize that there is no one thing such as *the* teaching personality, to be adopted by all people. Further than that, it would probably be rather deleterious to a person's teaching ability if he were asked to change his teaching personality and assume another. A sober-sided individual should not be a comedian, nor, on the other hand, can you channel a person with a genuine comic sense of humor and sense of effervescence and tell him that he must be Mr. Sobersides himself in the classroom. However, as is the case in many human endeavors, there are limits beyond which one cannot go and remain effective. Too much of the comic turns the teacher into an entertainer, too much of the sober-sides turns the students into a pack of bored animals. We could go on pointing out examples of going beyond these limits. But for our own purposes in this particular area, let us remember that one of the first considerations governing the choice of operation of the teacher is the teacher's assessment of his own personality.

These have been rather exhortatory phrases, somewhat on the cliché level. However, there has been some investigation in the field of leadership in social psychology that has pertinence here.

One of the classic studies is the Lewin, Lippit, and White studies of autocratic, democratic, laissez-faire leadership patterns. Operating with early teen-agers in work-producing tasks, the investigators set up three leadership roles: autocratic—the children were given no choice, no sense of ultimate directions to their work but, rather, were given close directions for immediate activities; democratic—the children were given several choices of direction, supporting directions for their tasks, a sense of reward, and also reproof; laissez-faire—the students were given little sense of directions for their tasks and little sense of their goals and were given a great deal of freedom of choice as to their behavior and goals. The investigators found that the pattern of behaviors called democratic resulted in the most work and the work atmosphere that seemed "best" in that it was free of the repression that characterized the autocratic and the many skirmishes that characterized the insecurity of the laissez-faire. Lest you think that there is an element here of the self-fulfillment prophecy, let it be said, hastily, that neither the leaders nor the children ever heard the roles referred to by name.

Other characteristics of leadership have been explored scientifically by social psychologists and more emotionally in literature. (*Hamlet can* be read as a study of man assuming a needed leadership but it is to be hoped that it will be read for more.) If there is a common thread to this it is that there seem to be two main leadership roles, the natural leader and the designated leader. Of course, the greatest group movement will take place when one person assumes both, but a movement of the group can take place under either. Suffice it to say that the instructor *is* the designated leader of his group. His teaching personality must take this into account and it is to be hoped his personality will also assume the natural role.

**The Subject to be Taught.** The next consideration governing the choice of the mode of operation is probably even more important. That is the type of subject matter to be taught at the particular moment. What kind of a search image is going into the system? The type of search image, the content of the search image, the domain in which the search image lies, very often become the criteria for the mode of operation that is going to be followed. Again, we refer to the chart of elements of the parts of the system that has been developed in earlier chapters in this book to which we added the modes of operation of the teacher in this chapter. Not only is it necessary to examine what type of search image is in the chart but it is also necessary to examine what might be called the emotional load of the search image to be presented to the student. What is its intrinsic worth? Is it a subject of major importance? Is it a subject of minor importance? Is it illustrative? Is it substantive? Does it have within it elements of controversy, elements about which the society itself has not made up its mind? These considerations define what we might call emotional load. It almost goes without saying that those subjects with a higher emotional load demand a little bit different type of treatment than those with a lower emotional load. It might be a little bit wild in a classroom to have students start out an examination of information on the speculative level of something that has a very high emotional load. People soon fall into the pattern of shedding more heat than light on the subject and what starts out to be in the instructor's mind as a calm search for knowledge, a calm search for conciliation of points of view, turns into a highly charged, emotional scramble between minds which immediately take on an adversary point of view.

**The Learner in the System.** A third consideration governing the choice of modes of operation in the strategic development of the subject matter in the classroom lies in the type of learner who happens to be in the class. There are many considerations here and they lie at the confluence of the psychological background of the student and the sociological background of the student that was discussed in Chapter 6 of this book. One of the first considerations, of course, is the social value system of the group of students. In broad terms, do these people follow the general middle-class social value system? Or are they of another group who has a different value system? Of course, different value systems will demand different means of operation on the subject matter.

The second consideration about the learners lies in the general developmental level of their minds. Are these people at the beginning stages of learning, are they just at the acquiring stage of learning the material? Is this the first time around, so to speak? Or have they had experience in the subject matter before so that they are now penetrating more deeply into the structure of the subject? These considerations, of course, make a difference in the mode of operation. Quite often it is advisable for the beginning person to start his study of the subject within the expository mode moving from that mode into the hypothetical and then into the speculative mode when he has had more experience in handling this particular type of subject matter. Conversely, if the student has had a good bit of experience with the subject matter and finds himself rather conversant with the subject matter, it might be well to start right in with the speculative area.

Another consideration is the intellectual ability of the student. This is not to say that slower students can work only at the expository level. Nor is to say that the speculative level should be reserved only for the fast student. What it means, of course, is the level of operation within any one of these modes of operation. The depth of penetration, the type of vocabulary used, the amount of time spent in developing concepts, are all going to be different when there are students of different intellectual abilities in a particular class.

**The Social-Emotional Climate.** All of this is the hollow tinkle of dissonant bells, of course, without adding to it the learner, his aims, his ambitions, his motivations, his power input into the system of instruction. A factor in the class situation that can very often determine the student's effort is what has come to be known as the social-emotional climate. It has been noted by many researchers that learning proceeds best in an atmosphere that is free from anxiety on the part of the students. This must be modified by staying free from unnatural anxieties. There is, of course, the natural anxiety of persons facing unknown learning tasks. But the unnatural anxiety of tensions caused by the teacher in a classroom do minimize the learning efforts of the students. There has been some good research done on the ways of observing and describing the teacher's contribution to the social-emotional climate in the classroom. The research of John Withall[4] maintains that:

> Each teacher-statement contains one of two dominant kinds of intent. These are:
> a) intent to sustain the teacher and his behavior (teacher-centered statements) or
> b) intent to sustain the learner and his behavior (learner-centered statements and issue-centered statements are included under this intent).
>
> By analysis of both the CONTEXT and the CONTENT of a teacher statement it may be possible to determine whether the dominant intent of a statement is to sustain the teacher or the learner.
>
> Once the dominant intent of a teacher-statement has been ascertained, one can proceed to determine the technique by which the support is conveyed.
>
> 1. If the statement is intended primarily to *sustain the teacher*, one or possibly a combination of the two following techniques may be used:
> a) reproof of the learner (category 6),
> b) directing or advising the learner (category 5).
>
> Frequently the intent of the statements is to sustain the teacher yet neither of the above techniques is used. In that event the statement is simply a self-supportive remark which defends the teacher or evidences perseveration in support of the teacher's position or ideas (category 7).
>
> 2. If the intent of a statement is to *sustain the learner* then one or possibly a combination of the two following techniques may be used:
> a) clarification and acceptance of the learner's feeling or ideas (category 2),
> b) problem-structuring statements (category 3).
>
> Frequently the intent of a statement is to sustain the learner yet neither of the above techniques is used. In that event the statement is simply one that reassures, commends, agrees with or otherwise sustains the learner (category 1).
>
> Infrequently a teacher-statement may have no dominant intent to sustain either the teacher or the learner. If the statement represents neither of the techniques in the two intent areas nor gives evidence of being one of the more general kinds of supporting statements, then the statement can be considered to have no intent to support and should be placed in category 4.

[4] John Withall, "The Development of a Technique for the Measurement of Social-Emotional Climate in Classrooms," *Journal of Experimental Education*, XVIII, 3 (March, 1949). These ideas have been amplified in many personal discussions that are gratefully acknowledged.

Recourse to the learner-statement or behavior before and after a teacher response, particularly when one encounters a statement in which the intent is difficult to ascertain, is sometimes helpful in categorizing the teacher's statements.

## CRITERIA OF TEACHER-STATEMENT CATEGORIES

1. LEARNER-SUPPORTIVE statements or questions. These are teacher-statements or questions that express agreement with the ideas, actions or opinions of the learner, or that commend or reassure the learner. Agreement is frequently expressed by a monosyllabic response such as "Yes," "Right," "Uhuhuh," and the like. Commendation or reassurance may be stated in terms of:

   a) class-accepted criteria or goals or
   b) the private goals and subjective criteria of the teacher.

The *dominant intent* of these statements or questions is to *praise, encourage,* or *bolster* the learner.

2. ACCEPTANT or CLARIFYING statements or questions. These are teacher-statements or questions which either:

   a) accept, that is, evidence considerable understanding by the teacher of, or
   b) clarify, that is, restate clearly and succinctly in the teacher's words

the ideational or the feeling content of the learner's statement. The *dominant* intent of these teacher-responses is to help the learner to gain insight into his problem, that is, define his "real" problem and its solution in more operational terms.

3. PROBLEM-STRUCTURING statements or questions. Problem-structuring responses by the teacher offer facts or ideas or opinions to the learner about a) phenomena and b) procedures in a non-threatening and objective manner. These responses contain NO element or advising or recommending the adoption of certain ideas or procedures. Problem-structuring responses are frequently posed as questions which seek further information from the learner about the problem confronting him; or they may be statements which offer information to the learner about his problem. The learner is free to accept or to reject in part or in entirety the facts or opinions that are presented to him. Problem-structuring responses may be questions which the teacher asks (1) to further increase her own understanding of what the learner has said, or (2) to increase the precision of the learner's statement of the problem. Problem-structuring responses are problem-centered rather than either teacher or learner-centered; nevertheless, they do tend to sustain the learner by facilitating his problem-solving activities.

4. NEUTRAL statements evidencing no supportive intent. These statements are neither teacher-sustaining, nor learner-sustaining nor problem-centered. They constitute a small percentage of the total teacher-responses. These responses include statements in which the teacher: (1) questions herself aloud; (2) repeats verbatim a statement that the learner just made; (3) uses a polite formality; et cetera. Statements having to do with administrative procedure—the room in which the class will meet, the hour at which a conference will occur—(especially after consensus has been achieved), fall into this category.

5. DIRECTIVE statements or questions. These are teacher-statements or questions which advise the learner regarding a course of action or his future behavior and which narrowly limit his choice or offer no choice. These statements recommend to the learner the facts or procedures that the teacher proffers him. These statements or questions convey the impression to the learner that the teacher expects and hopes that he will follow her prompting and that she will approve if he does. The *intent* of these responses is to have the learner take up the teacher's point of view and pursue a course of action that she advocates.

6. REPROVING, DISAPPROVING, or DISPARAGING statements or questions. By means of these statements a teacher may express a complete or partial disapproval of the ideas, behavior, and, to her, personality weaknesses of the learner. The teacher's internalized societal values largely enter into these responses. By means of these statements some teachers believe they are fulfilling their responsibility of inculcating in young people society's standards of acceptable and desirable behavior and achievement. The *intent* of these statements is:

a) to represent to the learner societal values as the teacher sees them;

b) to admonish the learner for unacceptable behavior and to deter him from repeating it in the future;

c) to impress on the learner the fact that he has not met the criteria for successful achievement which the teacher accepts.

7. TEACHER-SUPPORTIVE statements or questions. These are statements or questions in which the teacher refers to herself and expresses a defensive attitude, or refers to her present or past interests, activities, or possessions with the purpose of reassuring herself and of confirming her position or her ideas in the eyes of those around her. The *dominant intent* of these teacher-responses is to *assert*, to *defend* or to *justify* the teacher. Statements in which the teacher perseverates on an idea, a belief or a suggestion would fall in this category.

By "perseveration" is meant a persisting in, a reiteration of, and a rigid advocacy of an idea or opinion by the teacher despite additional data being presented to her which calls for a re-examination of the original idea or opinion.

These seven categories define a pattern for observation of teachers' verbal behaviors that presumably affect the social-emotional atmosphere. The research that established these criteria tended to prove that pupil-supportive acts by the teacher enhanced learning in the class. Students apparently feel a sense of accomplishment in their learning task and a sense of support for what they are doing when the teacher, through these verbal acts, acts in a pupil-supportive manner. Apparently when a teacher acts in a teacher-supportive manner the pupil feels excluded from the dialog and, if we accept the idea that instruction is a dialog between teacher and student, this feeling of exclusion would certainly mitigate against the necessary communication and, therefore, against learning. It becomes a rule of thumb, therefore, that the more that the teacher operates in the pupil-supportive area, the more the social-emotional climate of the classroom is conducive to learning. In this way, the teacher operates through the affective domain to get at the cognitive domain of his instruction.

These, then, are the general considerations of what kind of a teacher he is, of what kind of a search image there is in the system at the particular moment, of what kind of learner he is dealing with at that particular moment in the system of instruction. These considerations must be taken into account as the teacher makes his choice of modes of operation that become the strategies that he employs in the instruction process in the classroom.

A further word about the instructor's verbal behavior in the classroom. This verbal behavior discussion has to do with the instruction in the classroom. Studies have shown, however, that the system of instruction does not occupy the total amount of the teacher's time in the classroom. One study in particular by Smith has shown that as high as 30% of the teacher's verbal activities in the class were in the level of classroom management rather than of instruction. Classroom management verbal behavior has to do with such things as, "Sit down and shut up," "Don't move, the bell hasn't rung," "Willie, will you get your feet off the desk," and such other homilies as teachers feel called upon to utter to keep the students managed properly. This whole chapter, it must be emphasized, has been devoted to the strategies for instruction in a classroom, and it does not take into account strategies for manipulation of the management factors in a classroom. It doesn't seem possible to discuss these without knowing the context of the teacher's background, of the students' background, and the explicit situations demanding analyses unless we descend to a cookbook-recipe level of operation. For the new teachers, let us remember that these strategies are for instruction and that when he does get into his own classroom he will have to find his own patterns of classroom management, and that these patterns will come to him almost intuitively while he is at work in the classroom. They do enter into the system of instruction, because they often form part of the class personality and the teacher's personality which, as we have tried to point out, do have an effect on the choice of modes of operation in the classroom.

## SOME DIALOGS AND THE CHARTING THEREOF

These strategies for classroom behavior can be observed and charted. However, it must be pointed out that it is easier to define the strategies that the teacher employs in the cognitive domain of his teaching than in the affective domain. As can be seen on the above criteria of teacher-statement categories, much of the determination of category is dependent upon factors that are not demonstrated in an examination of the written word. Facial expression, tone of voice, physical actions of both instructor and learner, must be taken into account in any attempt to place statements into one of the seven categories.

In the cognitive domain, the written word in the reproduction of the dialog more faithfully mirrors the actual dialog, and it is much easier to categorize these statements.

Four simulated dialogs of examination of search images in teaching episodes can serve as models for some of these ideas.

## First Dialog

$I_1$. John Marshall's court issued many decisions of far-reaching importance. One of the first and most important was *Marbury* v. *Madison*. So that we can understand the historical importance of the Marshall court, let's examine this case. Can anyone tell us the details of the case?

$L_1$. Well, Marbury received an appointment to become a government official and before the commission was signed by Jefferson he went out of office. So Marbury sued Madison, the next president, for it and the court said he could.

$I_2$. That's fine—you covered it well, but let's look into it a bit further. What was the court order called that Marbury wanted?

$L_2$. A writ of mandamus?

$I_3$. That's right. Now what is that?

$L_3$. An order from a judge to produce a criminal's body.

$I_4$. No. I think you're talking about a writ of habeas corpus. What is a writ of mandamus?

$L_4$. *(After some hesitation.)* That's when a judge orders a court to enforce its own decision.

$I_5$. Right, but why is that necessary? Isn't a court decision always carried out?

$L_5$. No.

$I_6$. Can you give an example?

$L_6$. The Supreme Court said there should not be segregation in the schools, but there is.

$I_7$. That's right. (*The teacher seems to have missed the point of "all deliberate speed."*) But back to the writ. Is there anything more?

$L_7$. Aha, yes. A court can be forced to issue an order to enforce a law.

$I_8$. By Jove, I do believe you've got it. Now, what principle of American government does this illustrate?

$L_8$. The federal-state relationship?

$L_9$. Oh no, how could it? What about the *courts?*

$L_9$. Oh, I know. The separation of powers between the legislators, the executive, and the courts?

$L_{10}$. No. Doesn't anyone see? The writ of mandamus shows the principle of a government of laws, not men. It means that laws govern men and that the court, being men, can be held accountable to law. That's the importance of a writ of mandamus, and that's what *Marbury* v. *Madison* is all about. Now, let's look at another of the decisions of Chief Justice. . . .

### TABLE 9–1
#### FIRST DIALOG

| Dialog Number | Cognitive | | Social-Emotional Climate |
|---|---|---|---|
| | Instructor | Learner | |
| 1 | De | Com (includes an error) | 3 |
| 2 | De | Com | 1,3 |
| 3 | De | Kn | 1,3 |
| 4 | De | Kn | 3,3 |
| 5 | Ex | Com | 1,3 |
| 6 | In | Ap | 3 |
| 7 | De | An | 1,3 |
| 8 | Ex | Ap | 1,3 |
| 9 | De | Ap | 3 |
| 10 | Ex | Ap | 6,3,4 |

| Describing | Knowledge | 1—learner-supportive |
|---|---|---|
| Explaining | Comprehension | 2—acceptant |
| Inferring | Application | 3—problem-structuring |
| Evaluating | Analysis | 4—neutral-class managing |
| | Synthesis | 5—directive |
| | | 6—reproving, disapproving |
| | | 7—teacher-supportive |

In this first dialog the instructor's verbal acts were primarily of the descriptive nature with a little of explanation (see Table 9–1). These in turn elicited generally descriptive responses from the learners. The whole episode seemed to be little more than a descriptive recital of student's previously memorized ideas. The whole performance seems to be faintly reminiscent of tinkling bells and salivating dogs. Neither the learner nor the instructor seems to realize that, not only was the process sterile, but the learning itself is wrong.

#### SECOND DIALOG

$I_1$. Now, class, for our understanding of underdeveloped nations and why they are that way, let us look at the *sertão* of Brazil. Here on the map up here is the area—it is in the northeast of the country along about here (*indicating its general area with a sweep of the hand*). Now you're all tenth graders and can presumably read a map. From the map, Willie, can you tell me something about this area?

$L_1$. It's pretty big.

$I_2$. That's right, it is rather extensive. Anything else?

L₂. It seems to be a high plain.

I₃. High?

L₃. Well, higher than the coastline.

I₄. That's right, but let's look at another part of the geography. What about this small rainfall map here—what does that say to us?

L₄. There isn't any.

I₅. Any?

L₅. Well, very little.

I₆. That's right—it's a desert almost. But can it be a desert with this river running here (*pointing to the Rio São Francisco*)?

L₆. Sure, because it isn't a real desert. There just isn't enough regular rain.

I₇. That's right, it's desert like the American southwest rather than the Sahara. But let's turn to another side of the picture—the economic. Your text doesn't say much about this so let me make a few points about it. The major thing to understand is that it is a land of poverty. The annual income is less than $30 per year. This is a grinding poverty that means there is little to buy or sell and that there is a direct consumption of food produced. The soil is poor; the farming methods are primitive so there is only a bare minimum produced. Much of the land is owned by someone from the cities, and these absentee landlords are not interested in improving things too much, generally speaking.

The people are poor and they have few schools. The illiteracy rate is very high and so is the birth rate. They are superstitious and have a mystique about their land. During the many dry years there will be quite a migration out of the *sertão* to the big cities of the south and coast. Then when the rains return (as they must by the law of averages) the word seems to get around, and the people begin to return to the *sertão*. Even though it is a completely marginal land, they have the feeling that it will be good someday. So they keep on. This is a land of legends. The men are often *vaqueiros* riding after scrawny cattle through the *caatinga*, a scrubby plant with a spiny growth much like our mesquite in the west.

L₇. This seems to be like the west in our country with cowboys and everything. Don't you suppose that it will naturally change into something good as our west did?

I₈. That is an analogy that is made often, but I don't think that it is a good one. For one thing, the American west didn't have much population and this does—about 40,000,000. To make the analogy correct you would have to have 40,000,000 people in Utah, Arizona, Nevada, and New Mexico. So, Mr. Teacher-trapper, you didn't trap me after all.

But what does all this add up to?

L₈. I guess that this part of Brazil is underdeveloped because it doesn't have much rain and the people are poor and illiterate.

I$_9$. That's right as far as it goes, but let's not get trapped into thinking that there is a connection between rain and development. The connection is between geographic base and development, and rainfall is only a part of that base.

Now what are some other factors that cause underdevelopment? Are there any questions?

TABLE 9–2
SECOND DIALOG
Verbal Behavior Classification

| Dialog Number | Cognitive | | Social-Emotional Climate |
|---|---|---|---|
| | Instructor | Learner | |
| 1 | In | Com | 4,3,6,3 |
| 2 | In | Ap | 1,3 |
| 3 | Ex | Ap | 3 |
| 4 | In | Ap | 1,3 |
| 5 | Ex | Ap | 3 |
| 6 | Ev | Ap | 1,3 |
| 7 | Ex | Syn | 1,4,3,3 |
| 8 | In, Ev | Syn | 3,3,2 |
| 9 | Ex | — | 1,3 |

| | | |
|---|---|---|
| Describing | Knowledge | 1—learner-supportive |
| Explaining | Comprehension | 2—acceptant |
| Inferring | Application | 3—problem-structuring |
| Evaluating | Analysis | 4—neutral-class managing |
| | Synthesis | 5—directive |
| | Evaluation | 6—reproving, disapproving |
| | | 7—teacher-supportive |

In this second dialog the instructor's verbal acts were of such a nature as to invite a great deal more involvement of the learners' minds (Table 9–2). The acts were preponderantly of the explaining or inferring level and called forth responses of the same type. Much more involvement of active minds is evidenced here than in the first dialog.

In so doing the classroom social-emotional climate seemed to be "warm" with many verbal acts, of both instructor and learner, being on the learner-supportive level.

### THIRD DIALOG

I$_1$. In our continuing discussion of civil rights and responsibilities let's look at another one. I have here a clipping that says that a government official is proposing that all of the information about each person in the U.S. that is contained in various agencies be brought together and stored in a giant computer where it could be recalled at any time. What do you think about this?

$L_1$. It seems to be a good idea.

$I_2$. Why?

$L_2$. Well, all of the stuff needed would be in one spot.

$L_3$. Why is this information needed?

$L_{3(1)}$. So that the people that need to know can know what they need to know.

$L_{3(2)}$. Yeah, but why do they need to know?

$L_{3(3)}$. Maybe I don't want them to know something about me!

$L_{3(4)}$. *(General murmurings of chidings of ill will about what he has done that should be secret.)*

$I_4$. Let's look at this a moment. We're just airing opinions now; perhaps we can do more. Let's put them together into an examination of something. What is the problem posed by this use of the computer?

$L_4$. Everybody will know everybody's secrets.

$I_5$. Perhaps that is an overgeneralization; perhaps it could be phrased a little better. What civil right seems to be endangered?

$L_5$. Freedom of speech?

$I_6$. No.

$L_6$. Freedom of assembly?

$I_7$. No, and I think that you are guessing. One of the Congressmen said that this is an invasion of personal privacy. Willie?

$L_{7(1)}$. I read about that in some magazines where they were talking about all the bugs in rooms.

$L_{7(2)}$. Oh yeah, where the olive in the martini is a radio that sends a message.

$L_{7(3)}$. I seen a movie where a girl had a microphone in her—

$I_8$. *(Interrupting hastily for he, too, had seen the film and where the microphone was hidden.)* There has been a lot of discussion about the use of these electronic devices. But— Yes, Willie?

$L_8$. Can the police tap the telephones?

$I_9$. Do you mean "can" or "may"?

$L_9$. It doesn't make much difference. *Can* they?

$I_{10}$. It does make a difference. It is possible to do it but whether they have permission to do it or not is another question.

$L_{10}$. Well, do they?

$I_{11}$. They do, but they are not always supposed to. Now what about the hypothesis: is this an invasion of the right of privacy?

$L_{11}$. How do these computers work?

$I_{12}$. Don't be impertinent, young man. Answer the question.

$L_{12}$. Yes, teacher, it is an invasion of the right of privacy.

$I_{13}$. You're right. It has been called that. Can you tell me why you answered it that way?

L$_{13}$. (*In a voice audible only to his classmates.*) Because that's the answer you wanted.

I$_{14}$. (*With professional cheeriness.*) The bell will ring soon, so that's all for today. Tomorrow we will discuss one of our most valuable freedoms—freedom of speech.

TABLE 9–3
THIRD DIALOG
Verbal Behavior Classification

| Dialog Number | Cognitive | | Social-Emotional Climate |
| | Instructor | Learner | |
|---|---|---|---|
| 1 | De | Ev | 4,3 |
| 2 | Ev | An | 3 |
| 3 | Ev | Ap, An, Ev | 3 |
| 4 | Ev | Syn | 5,3,5,3 |
| 5 | In | Kn | 3 |
| 6 | Ev | Kn | 3 |
| 7 | Ev | Ap, Ap, Ap | 6,4 |
| 8 | De | Ap | 6 |
| 9 | De | Ev | 3 |
| 10 | De | Ev | 3 |
| 11 | De, Ev | Com | 3 |
| 12 | De | Com | 2,5 |
| 13 | Ex | Ev | 1,3 |
| 14 | De | | 4 |

| Describing | Knowledge | 1—learner-supportive |
| Explaining | Comprehension | 2—acceptant |
| Inferring | Application | 3—problem-structuring |
| Evaluating | Analysis | 4—neutral-class managing |
| | Synthesis | 5—directive |
| | Evaluation | 6—reproving, disapproving |
| | | 7—teacher-supportive |

An interesting phenomenon is apparent in this dialog. The analysis of the verbal activity (Table 9–3) shows that for about the first half of the episode the acts were on a level of involvement of learner minds. At the same time the social-emotional climate seemed to be learner-supportive.

Then at about the seventh interchange something happened to this pattern. The learners' minds began to get caught up in the illustration, rather than the substance. Subsequent interchanges reveal that they seemed bound to discuss "bugging" rather than invasions of privacy, let alone computer storage of statistics. The general recalcitrance at the instructor's tugging shows itself in the social-emotional climate; it shifts over to teacher supportive. At the same time, the mental involvement of the learners drops off to the sheer descriptive level. So toward the last they are doing what the instructor demands, rather than what the subject demands.

### Fourth Dialog

The fourth dialog is an example of how the instructor's decision can vary the mode of operation. This same subject could be presented as a logically demonstrable type on the expository level as "The Election of 1960." It also could have been of the postulate type on the hypothetical mode of operation, "The election results in 1960 were such that President Kennedy had little mandate for change and thus little change happened." In this dialog the instructor chose to operate on the speculative mode as the class examines the postulate, "Kennedy could not have been elected in 1960 if Stevenson had not been the candidate in 1952 and 1956."

$I_1$. Class, here on the board is a sentence. As you can see, it is not absolutely provable—no one can say that it is completely true or false. But it is well worth looking at. We are not so much interested in facts to be memorized as we are in bringing the facts together into a logical thought process. So let us speculate about this. What does this statement compare?

$L_1$. It doesn't compare anything.

$I_2$. I mean, what does it ask you to compare as you think about it?

$L_2$. Kennedy and Stevenson?

$I_3$. That's right. But before we compare them what else is in that statement on the board? It has to do with the comparison of time.

$L_3$. I guess the elections of 1952, '56, and '60.

$I_4$. That's right—you people deserve the reputation of being a good group. Now comes the key question. Should we look for likenesses or differences between Stevenson and Kennedy?

$L_4$. Likenesses.

$I_5$. That's right; you're very good. Why did you say that?

$L_5$. (Sheepishly.) I just guessed.

$I_6$. (Lamely amidst laughter.) Well, it was a good guess. (Recovering.) It was a good guess but right because, according to the postulate, Kennedy built on Stevenson. Or another way of saying it, Stevenson paved the way. So voters looked for similar things. So what were these likenesses?

$L_6$. Excuse me for saying this, but I hardly remember Kennedy and I don't remember Stevenson at all. All I can remember of the 1956 election is that we voted in the third grade and Eisenhower won.

$I_7$. Oh, I guess I had forgotten how young the young are—or how old I am. What does the book say?

$L_{7(1)}$. Very little about Stevenson except that he was governor of Illinois.

$L_{7(2)}$. And that nobody could have won against Eisenhower.

$L_{7(3)}$. It doesn't say that; it just says that Eisenhower was a very popular war hero and that after every war but one we had elected one.

$L_{7(2)}$. Well, I was just practicing what the teacher calls "inference."

$I_8$. That's what he was doing. I guess the book doesn't help us here so let me add what I can. It seems to me that where Stevenson and Kennedy were alike was in their feeling for the intellect. Both of them were expert in the use of words; their speeches are marvelous reading. In fact, Stevenson spent so much time polishing his speeches that his aides often despaired. They thought he was neglecting the other parts of campaigning. This characteristic of his—his intellectual quality—often was used against him. He was called an "egghead." To many people in that time there was something wrong in being interested in the world of ideas, in using graceful words. His defense against this was often a merry quip. One of his comments was "Eggheads of the world unite—you have nothing to lose but your yolks." And another time speaking at Harvard, in March, 1964.

> Confronted, surrounded indeed, as I am here in Cambridge tonight by more highly educated fellow citizens than I have ever faced, and inadequately prepared, I am uncomfortably reminded of the abiding truth of those classic words that never occurred to Horace: *"Via ovicipitum dura est,"* or for the benefit of the engineers among you: "The way of the egghead is hard."

$L_8$. He seemed to be quite a wit. Wasn't—didn't Kennedy make a lot of jokes, too?

$I_9$. Certainly. Since his death there have been many collections published containings his jokes and quips.

$L_9$. Tell us some of them.

$I_{10}$. There goes the bell. I'll save them for tomorrow.

TABLE 9–4
FOURTH DIALOG
Verbal Behavior Classification

| Dialog Number | Cognitive | | Social-Emotional Climate |
|---|---|---|---|
| | Instructor | Learner | |
| 1 | Ev, In | An | 3 |
| 2 | In | An | 3 |
| 3 | In | An | 1,3 |
| 4 | In | An | 1,3 |
| 5 | Ev | An | 1,3 |
| 6 | In | Com | 2,3 |
| 7 | Ev, De | Com, Com, An, Com | 7,3 |
| 8 | Ex | Com | 1,3 |
| 9 | De | Kn | 1,3 |
| 10 | De | — | 4 |

| | | |
|---|---|---|
| Describing | Knowledge | 1—learner-supportive |
| Explaining | Comprehension | 2—acceptant |
| Inferring | Application | 3—problem-structuring |
| Evaluating | Analysis | 4—neutral-class managing |
| | Synthesis | 5—directive |
| | Evaluation | 6—reproving, disapproving |
| | | 7—teacher-supportive |

Analysis of this fourth dialog shows that all seems to be going well (Table 9–4). The instructor and learner verbal activity seems to be at a level that involves the minds in something more than a memorization-regurgitation exercise. The social-emotional climate seems to be somewhat learner supportive. The whole thing seems to be rather genial and warm with instructor and learner in happy pursuit of the search image through an examination of the postulate.

However, there is a black cloud on the horizon. Somehow in this mental involvement the search image seems to shift to a discussion of the Stevensonian wit.

There seems to be this phenomenon in the instructional process. The minds in the system, the instructor's and the learners', can act on the image in such a way that it begins to change. It is to an examination of this phenomenon that we turn next.

## SUGGESTED READINGS

BELLACK, ARNO. "The Language of the Classroom," Cooperative Research Project No. 2023, Institute of Psychological Research, Teachers College, Columbia University, 1965.

FLANDERS, NED A. *Teacher Influence, Pupil Attitudes, and Achievement,* Cooperative Research No. 12, U.S. Office of Education.

GAGE, N. L. *Handbook of Research on Teaching* of American Educational Research Association, Part III (Chicago: Rand McNally & Company, 1963).

MITZEL, HAROLD E., and DONALD M. MEDLEY. "Measuring Classroom Behavior by Systematic Observation," in N. L. Gage, ed., *Handbook of Research on Teaching* of American Educational Research Association (Chicago: Rand McNally & Company, 1963).

OLIVER, DONALD W., and JAMES P. SHAVER. *Teaching Public Issues in the High School* (Boston: Houghton Mifflin Company, 1966).

RIBBLE, ROBERT B. "The Structure-Discovery Approach in the Social Studies," Unpublished dissertation, Ohio State University, 1966.

SANDERS, NORRIS M. *Classroom Questions, What Kinds?* (New York: Harper & Row, Publishers, 1966).

# chapter TEN

# Action of Minds on Ideas

*The more you think, plan, and organize, the more things will be different, anyway.*—Searles' Law.

The quote that provides the theme for this chapter has been found to be rather apt and it is freely admitted that the author holds no private monopoly on the sentiment expressed. Others may have found the same law to be operative in their own personal patterns of life.

Let it serve as a gentle warning for all those who want to enter the patterns of instruction. Though the law operates in any area of human endeavor, instruction seems to be peculiarly subject to uncertainty and change. There is a certain inherent problem about the process that is rather analogous to what physical scientists have learned to call "the uncertainty principle." They maintain that anything in the physical world that is under observation changes its characteristics. In the same way, we find that any search image that is under observation by the instructor and the learner in the system of instruction tends to change its characteristics under the impact of the minds that operate upon that particular search image in that system of instruction.

## THE DESCRIPTION OF THE VARIATION

This variable of the action of minds and ideas is one over which the teacher has very little control. It can be best defined by an examination of that part of the model of the system of instruction which has been labeled "perception screens."

**Perception Screens.** The whole background of the learner and of the instructor including their emotional makeup, their experience background, their apperceptive mass, their whole total personalities becomes the screen through which each perceives his world. This background tends to surround him, if you can accept the change in metaphors, and acts as a filter or screen through which he views and understands this world. In the system of instruction he sends his messages through this screen. That is to say that, when the teacher enters the system of instruction with a search image, that search image is going to be perceived by that teacher in a certain way that is thoroughly defined by his perception screen. As the student or as the learner operates from the other side of the system and is motivated to reach up to the search image toward an understanding of the search image, he operates through his own perception screen, and thus does not always see the search image in the same way as the teacher means that he should see it.

In this particular sense, "see" really means "perceive." It is more than an actual visual process; it is a process of the mind's seeing or, in more precise terms, of the mind's perceiving what that search image is. Two stories, perhaps apocryphal, illustrate this idea of perception screens.

During World War II the U.S. Navy had a station in a village in the interior of China (Don't ask what the Navy was doing in the interior of China; that isn't the point) that was rather beset by disease. So the sailors there embarked on an instructional campaign to rid the area of many of the flies. In the best pedagogical fashion they set out to show the locals why they should kill flies. They brought in a movie projector and screen and projected a detailed drawing of a fly to show how germs are carried in the filth trapped on the legs. When the picture appeared, the audience walked out amidst uproarious laughter. Then the befuddled sailors found the reason: there are no flies that large; the Americans were being silly again. The locals didn't know the principles of enlargement and projection and couldn't perceive the idea of a fly that large.

A team of health workers were conducting a campaign in Africa to improve the nutrition of the natives. They found that chickens were being killed and eaten before they had attained a full growth. A few weeks more of fattening would have added much to the ultimate nutritional value. So they brought in a movie projector and screen and that night in the village square showed a film replete with fat chickens and happy eaters. The next day they noticed many of the natives searching through the bushes near the square; they were looking for the fat chickens that were there the night before.

**Distortions of the Search Image.** This problem of each person's having to view the search image through his own perception screen leads to a certain tension in the system of instruction. This tension, as is the case in many physical tensions, tends to have a distorting effect on the search image as each participant twists and turns the image.

The search image may be such a simple thing as a description of a rose. Even there, the teacher can establish a distorted search image of that rose because of his own background experiences that have, for him, labeled the rose as being good. It smells good, it looks good, it has a romantic quality to it. As he describes the word "rose," he remembers a poetic phrase about the one perfect rose mirroring love, and things of that nature. If, at the same time, the student is perceiving "rose" through his own pattern of background which includes such things as brambles, thorns, stickers, hay fever, and allergies, he is going to be hard put to perceive "rose" in the same light that the teacher perceives "rose." There tends to be a tension as both struggle toward a common definition of this search image, a tension that leads to lack of coherence and of subsequent distortion of the search image in the mind.

**The Feedback in the System.** This quality must be accounted for in the system of instruction, and this in turn leads us to the bottom line in the model of the system of instruction—the direct line between the learner's mind and the instructor's mind. This is the line that acts as the feedback channel, and it is through this feedback channel that the perception of the search image that is building up in the learner's mind is judged by the instructor. It is through the feedback channel that the instructor judges the trial response of the learner, and it is through the feedback channel that the instructor evaluates the amount of distortion and coherence that the learner has of that particular search image.

This is not an easy ability to develop, and it is one of those areas in the system of instruction that demands a high degree of artistry by the instructor; it is here that the instructor knows that teaching is an art as well as a science.

The phenomenon can be described in the rather inelegant phrase, "teaching by the seat of the pants." Years ago when men were first trying out their flying machines, they learned to tell which way was up by judging a sensation flowing from the end of the spine not generally associated with the mind. In the same way, the teacher teaches by the seat of his pants; that is to say, he develops an intuitive sense of when things are on an even keel, when things are in a state of distortion. He develops it by the use of the feedback mechanism.

Experienced teachers find that, while one part of the mind is busily engaged in the forward-proceeding process of developing the structure of the subject matter, another part of the mind is acting in a little more of a judgmental sense. It is not proceeding so much as it is evaluating the feedback mechanism. A radarlike process operates here; that is to say that one part of the teacher's mind is sending out "a radar impulse," the other part of the teacher's mind is receiving that impulse a few seconds later and evaluating it, judging it, and perhaps reading it as blips on the radar screen of his mind. This feedback is in turn fed into the teacher's operational pattern and shapes that operational pattern back to the original search image pattern.

Again we may refer for an analogy to the communication pattern as developed in the previous chapter. In a way, the feedback returns through the same channels by which it was sent, and the teacher shapes his next action on the basis of the feedback that he received.

To add further inelegance to this particular pattern, the teacher must learn how not to beat on a dead horse. This homely phrase is a definition of a phenomenon in the system that occurs when further input brings a lesser return in learning. The instructor, through the feedback mechanism, can determine a point of diminishing returns for his effort in the instruction process.

This is the definition of the variable of the action of minds on ideas. It concerns itself primarily with the perception screens that surround the minds of the learner and of the teacher.

## CHOICES FOR THE INSTRUCTOR

There are certain choices, of course, that the teacher can make in this particular realm to vary the action of minds on ideas. They can best be defined by a chart or a model of the struggle for coherence and the temptation of distortion.

**The Struggle for Coherence and the Temptation of Distortion.**   Some definitions are in order. Coherence in this sense means a unity along the subject line that is consistent in its following of the structure. Distortion results when this is not followed.

While learners are led to the threshold of their own minds in a dialog, a certain pattern is formed. This journey can be mapped and the resulting chart or model will show the struggle for coherence and the temptation of distortion during that journey.

Basic to this discussion is the idea of a noise threshold. This idea is inspired in good part by the concept of noise discussed in the preceding chapter. The noise threshold is that point in a dialog wherein noise enters into the pattern and prevents the necessary communication from taking place. So in the model of the coherence and distortion in teaching that is being developed we place boundary lines on either side; one is the noise threshold of the teacher, the other is the noise threshold of the learner. At the top of the model is the entry of the search image. At the bottom of the model is the destination of the search image in the student's mind. The dialog proceeds through a channel bounded on either side by these noise thresholds. During the process, the search image is subject to distortions brought about by actions of the minds of the instructor and the students.

## SOME DIALOGS AND THE CHARTING THEREOF

So let us look at the simulated dialogs that we considered in Chapter 9, and then see if we can chart the progression of instructors and learners through them. For the sake of convenience in reference, the diaolgs are reproduced below.

### FIRST DIALOG

I₁. John Marshall's court issued many decisions of far-reaching importance. One of the first and most important was *Marbury* v. *Madison*. So that we can understand the historical importance of the Marshall court, let's examine this case. Can anyone tell us the details of the case?

L₁. Well, Marbury received an appointment to become a government official and before the commission was signed by Jefferson he went out of office. So Marbury sued Madison, the next president, for it and the court said he could.

I₂. That's fine—you covered it well, but let's look into it a bit further. What was the court order called that Marbury wanted?

L₂. A writ of mandamus?

I₃. That's right. Now what is that?

L₃. An order for a judge to produce a criminal's body.

I₄. No. I think you're talking about a writ of habeas corpus. What is a writ of mandamus?

L₄. *(After some hesitation.)* That's when a judge orders a court to enforce its own decision.

I₅. Right, but when is that necessary? Isn't a court decision always carried out?

L₅. No.

I₆. Can you give an example?

L₆. The Supreme Court said there should not be segregation in the schools, but there is.

I₇. That's right. (*The teacher seems to have missed the point of "all deliberate speed."*) But back to the writ. Is there anything more?

L₇. Aha, yes. A court can be forced to issue an order to enforce a law.

I₈. By Jove, I do believe you've got it. Now, what principle of American government does this illustrate?

L₈. The federal-state relationship?

I₉. Oh no, how could it? What about the *courts?*

L₉. Oh, I know. The separation of powers between the legislators, the executive, and the courts?

I₁₀. No. Doesn't anyone see? The writ of mandamus shows the principle of a government of laws, not men. It means that laws govern men and that the court, being men, can be held accountable to law. That's the importance of a writ of mandamus, and that's what *Marbury* v. *Madison* is all about. Now, let's look at another of the decisions of Chief Justice—

The first dialog—rather edited of vagaries of expression by instructor and learner—mirrored the mutual examination of the search image concerning judicial review. The dialog sounds good at first blush until the full realization hits us that it was the principle of judicial review that came forth in *Marbury* v. *Madison* rather than the importance of writs of mandamus, about which the dialog was mainly centered. Writs of mandamus were not an issue in this case; they were rather extraneous to it.

In our terminology, the parts did not add up to the whole. The infrastructure was wrong to the degree that the worst type of distortion took place: the learner was presented with a search image in which an extraneous issue became the central one. (To say nothing of the inaccuracies of the case itself.)

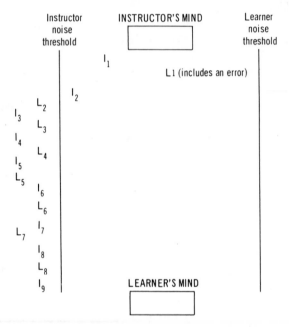

FIG. 10-1. Distortion of search image in the First Dialog.

This distortion is demonstrated on the chart of Fig. 10–1. It graphically shows the degree to which this search image has been changed by the action of minds on the idea. This dialog is in this sense a failure; the students learned the wrong thing. The distortion probably could be attributed to the instructor's ignorance; he obviously didn't know his subject and thus violated one of the cardinal principles of teaching. He proceeded correctly—there seems to be an inductive pattern formed—but to the wrong destination.

### Second Dialog

I₁. Now, class, for our understanding of underdeveloped nations and why they are that way, let us look at the *sertão* of Brazil. Here on the map up here is the area—it is in the northeast of the country along about here (*indicating its general area with a sweep of the hand*). Now you're all tenth graders and can presumably read a map. From the map, Willie, can you tell me something about this area?

L₁. It's pretty big.

I₂. That's right, it is rather extensive. Anything else?

L₂. It seems to be a high plain.

I₃. High?

L₃. Well, higher than the coastline.

I₄. That's right, but let's look at another part of the geography. What about this small rainfall map here—what does that say to us?

L₄. There isn't any.

I₅. Any?

L₅. Well, very little.

I₆. That's right—it's a desert almost. But can it be a desert with this river running here (*pointing to the Rio São Francisco*)?

L₆. Sure, because it isn't a real desert. There just isn't enough regular rain.

I₇. That's right, it's desert like the American southwest rather than the Sahara. But let's turn to another side of the picture—the economic. Your text doesn't say much about this so let me make a few points about it. The major thing to understand is that it is a land of poverty. The annual income is less than $30 per year. This is a grinding poverty that means there is little to buy or sell and that there is a direct consumption of food produced. The soil is poor; the farming methods are primitive so there is only a bare minimum produced. Much of the land is owned by someone from the cities, and these absentee landlords are not interested in improving things too much, generally speaking.

The people are poor and they have few schools. The illiteracy rate is very high and so is the birth rate. They are superstitious and have a mystique about their land. During the many dry years there will be quite a migration out of the *sertão* to the big cities of the south and coast. Then when the rains return (as they must by the law of averages) the word seems to get around and the people begin to return to the *sertão*. Even though it is a completely marginal land, they have the feeling that it will be good someday. So they keep on. This is a land of legends. The men are often *vaqueiros* riding after scrawny cattle through the *caatinga*, a scrubby plant with a spiny growth much like our mesquite in the west.

$L_7$. This seems to be like the west in our country with cowboys and everything. Don't you suppose that it will naturally change into something good as our west did?

$I_8$. That is an analogy that is made often, but I don't think that it is a good one. For one thing, the American west didn't have much population and this does—about 40,000,000. To make the analogy correct you would have to have 40,000,000 people in Utah, Arizona, Nevada, and New Mexico. So, Mr. Teacher-trapper, you didn't trap me after all.

But what does this all add up to?

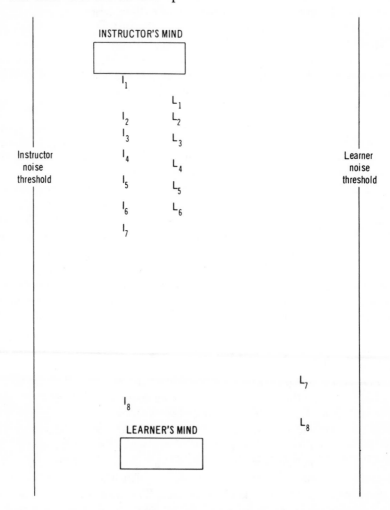

FIG. 10-2. Distortion and coherence of search image in the Second Dialog.

$L_8$. I guess that this part of Brazil is underdeveloped because it doesn't have much rain and the people are poor and illiterate.

$I_9$. That's right as far as it goes, but let's not get trapped into thinking that there is a connection between rain and development. The connection is between geographic base and development, and rainfall is only a part of that base.

Are there any questions?

Now what are some other factors that cause underdevelopment?

In this dialog the instructor proceded rather deductively. That is, he established the search image in the system in his opening statements and then, through this mutual examination, he and the learner's mind set about finding the support for it. In so doing there was a minimum of distortion and a maximum of coherence, as the chart of Fig. 10-2 shows. All of the dialog took place within limits prescribed by the subject as contrasted with the first dialog.

There was a temptation to go afield when Learner Response Seven came close to being noise. But the instructor recognized this and treated it properly. Rather than examining the American west and then comparing it, he showed it to be a rather weak analogy and went on with the dialog to the end that the structure of the idea of characteristics of underdeveloped areas was defined. It is practically impossible to judge from the bare bones of written dialog whether or not there was any discovery by the students. Vocal nuances and facial expressions must be judged as well to get a full measure of this side of instruction. We can see the structure forming, but only an actual physical presence in the dialog would allow the assessment of the discovery.

The general mode of operation here is expository; the questions interspersed seemed to be designed more to expose the structure than to challenge the mind. The mind involvement was on the product level rather than the process level.

### Third Dialog

$I_1$. In our continuing discussion of civil rights and responsibilities let's look at another one. I have here a clipping that says that a government official is proposing that all of the information about each person in the U.S. that is contained in various agencies be brought together and stored in a giant computer where it could be recalled at any time. What do you think about this?

$L_1$. It seems to be a good idea.

$I_2$. Why?

$L_2$. Well, all of the stuff needed would be in one spot.

$I_3$. Why is this information needed?

$L_{3(1)}$. So that the people who need to know can know what they need to know.

$L_{3(2)}$. Yeah, but why do they need to know?

$L_{3(3)}$. Maybe I don't want them to know something about me!

$L_{3(4)}$. (*General murmurings of chidings of ill will about what he has done that should be secret.*)

$I_4$. Let's look at this a moment. We're just airing opinions now; perhaps we can do more. Let's put them together into an examination of something. What is the problem posed by this use of the computer?

$L_4$. Everybody will know everybody's secrets.

$I_5$. Perhaps that is an overgeneralization; perhaps it could be phrased a little better. What civil right seems to be endangered?

$L_5$. Freedom of speech?

$I_6$. No.

$L_6$. Freedom of assembly?

$I_7$. No, and I think that you are guessing. One of the Congressmen said that this is an invasion of personal privacy. Willie?

$L_{7(1)}$. I read about that in some magazines where they were talking about all the bugs in rooms.

$L_{7(2)}$. Oh yeah, where the olive in the martini is a radio that sends a message.

$L_{7(3)}$. I seen a movie where a girl had a microphone in her—

$I_8$. (*Interrupting hastily for he, too, had seen the film and where the microphone was hidden.*) There has been a lot of discussion about the use of these electronic devices. But— Yes, Willie?

$L_8$. Can the police tap the telephones?

$I_9$. Do you mean "can" or "may"?

$L_9$. It doesn't make much difference. *Can* they?

$I_{10}$. It does make a difference. It is possible to do it, but whether they have permission to do it or not is another question.

$L_{10}$. Well, do they?

$I_{11}$. They do, but they are not always supposed to. Now what about the hypothesis: is this an invasion of the right of privacy?

$L_{12}$. How do these computers work?

$I_{13}$. Don't be impertinent, young man. Answer the question.

$L_{12}$. Yes, teacher, it is an invasion of the right of privacy.

$I_{13}$. You're right. It has been called that. Can you tell me why you answered it that way?

$L_{13}$. (*In a voice audible only to his classmates.*) Because that's the answer you wanted.

$I_{14}$. (*With professional cheeriness.*) The bell will ring soon, so that's all for today. Tomorrow we will discuss one of our most valuable freedoms— freedom of speech.

In the Third Dialog the instructor was operating in what we called the "hypothetical" mode. As charted in Fig. 10-3, he started on the limits of the subject, working with the introductory idea of the necessity for information, then into an examination of the hypothesis that the right of privacy was invaded. But in this subject there is a dramatic content that intrigued the minds—that of the electronic devices that are available for gathering informa-

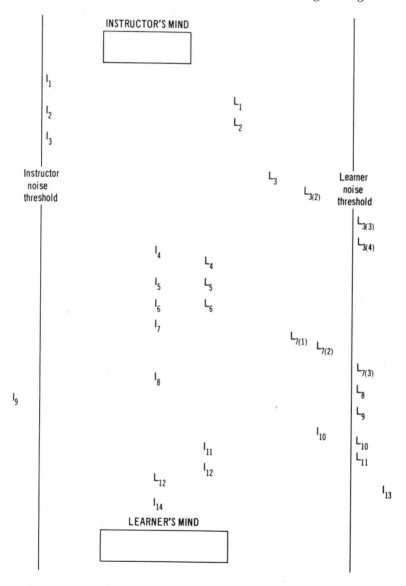

FIG. 10-3. Distortion and coherence of search image in the Third Dialog.

tion. This subject is alien to the idea of a central computer containing all of the information about everyone, but the electronic devices that gather information do provide another example of the abridgment of the right of privacy.

However, the instructor was able to get back to the original structure, albeit rather lamely.

## Fourth Dialog

$I_1$. Class, here on the board is a sentence. (Kennedy could not have been elected in 1960 if Stevenson hadn't run in 1952 and 1956.) As you can see, it is not absolutely provable—no one can say that it is completely true or false. But it is well worth looking at. We are not so much interested in facts to be memorized as we are in bringing the facts together into a logical thought process. So let us speculate about this. What does this statement compare?

$L_1$. It doesn't compare anything.

$I_2$. I mean, what does it ask you to compare as you think about it?

$L_2$. Kennedy and Stevenson?

$I_3$. That's right. But before we compare them what else is in that statement on the board. It has to do with the comparison of time.

$L_3$. I guess the elections of 1952, '56, and '60.

$I_4$. That's right—you people deserve the reputation of being a good group. Now come the key questions. Should we look for likenesses or differences between Stevenson and Kennedy?

$L_4$. Likenesses.

$I_5$. That's right; you're very good. Why did you say that?

$L_5$. (Sheepishly.) I just guessed.

$I_6$. (Lamely amidst laughter.) Well, it was a good guess. (Recovering.) It was a good guess but right because, according to the postulate, Kennedy built on Stevenson. Or another way of saying it, Stevenson paved the way. So voters looked for similar things. So what were these likenesses?

$L_6$. Excuse me for saying this, but I hardly remember Kennedy and I don't remember Stevenson at all. All I can remember of the 1956 election is that we voted in the third grade and Eisenhower won.

$I_7$. Oh, I guess I had forgotten how young the young are—or how old I am. What does the book say?

$L_{7(1)}$. Very little about Stevenson except that he was governor of Illinois.

$L_{7(2)}$. And that nobody could have won against Eisenhower.

$L_{7(3)}$. It doesn't say that; it just says that Eisenhower was a very popular war hero and that after every war but one we had elected one.

$L_{7(2)}$. Well, I guess I was just practicing what the teacher calls "inference."

$I_8$. That's what he was doing. I guess the book doesn't help us here so let me add what I can. It seems to me that where Stevenson and Kennedy were alike was in their feeling for the intellect. Both of them were expert in the use of words; their speeches are marvelous reading. In fact, Stevenson spent so much time polishing his speeches that his aides often despaired. They thought he was neglecting the other parts of campaigning. This characteristic of his—his intellectual quality—often was used against him. He was called an "egghead." To many people in that time there was something wrong in being interested in the world of ideas, in using graceful words. His defense against this was often a merry quip. One of his comments was "Eggheads of the world unite—you have nothing to lose but your yolks." And another time speaking at Harvard in March, 1964, he said,

> Confronted, surrounded indeed, as I am here in Cambridge tonight by more highly educated fellow citizens than I have ever faced, and inadequately prepared, I am uncomfortably reminded of the abiding truth of those classic words that never occurred to Horace: *"Via oviciputum dura est,"* or for the benefit of the engineers among you: "The way of the egghead is hard."

$L_8$. He seemed to be quite a wit. Wasn't—didn't Kennedy make a lot of jokes, too?

$I_9$. Certainly. Since his death there have been many collections published containing his jokes and quips.

$L_9$. Tell us some of them.

$I_{10}$. There goes the bell. I'll save them for tomorrow.

As shown on the model of the action of minds in Fig. 10-4 this dialog demonstrates how a mind can wander from one idea to another. At the start of Instructor Entry Eight, the instructor's mind was attentive to the idea of both candidates' allegiance to intellectual pursuits. Then, as his mind dwelled on the effect ("egghead") on the electorate, he began to slip away to the idea of wit as a defence and thence to wit as a characteristic of the two men. So the search image became distorted by the action of that mind.

Instructor Entry Five and the corresponding response is near the noise threshold because the instructor was moving from product to process even though in the initial entry he had shown that the major purpose was process.

Having examined this idea of distortion and coherence of an idea, a question arises. Some will say, "You mean a teacher shouldn't get off the subject? He shouldn't follow a student's mind and explore some extraneous but interesting idea?" (Of course, if he's capable of saying a sentence like *that*, he probably sees through the problem.) The idea of distortion and coherence does not mean that a teacher shouldn't get off the subject. What it does provide is a pattern by which a teacher can tell when he is leaving the subject and remind him of the dangers to the learning: that the learner will possibly get a distorted view of the idea and an incoherent structure of thought.

Parenthetically, it might be noted at this point that this idea of charting

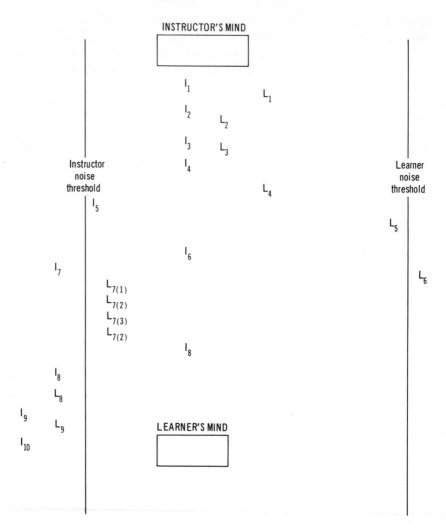

Fɪɢ. 10-4. Distortion and coherence of search image in the Fourth Dialog.

or modeling offers a very useful way for observing a classroom situation and a teacher's operation. It is quite difficult for a teacher, at a given time, to chart the progress of a search image through this channel but it is a simple matter for an observer in a classroom to so chart and it is not a very difficult task for a teacher to keep this chart in mind as a search image as he teaches and be able to judge when the action of the minds, either his or his learners, distorts the search image by taking it over the noise threshold. His choices, then, become choices of operation, choices of words, choices of thoughts that stay within this channel between these noise thresholds.

## CONSIDERATIONS GOVERNING THE INSTRUCTOR'S CHOICE

There seems to be some considerations that have to be taken into account as the teacher makes these choices of operation. We have spoken about the action of minds on ideas. The major consideration governing instructor's choices, thus becomes the consideration of the minds themselves, what types of minds there really are. This seems to be an almost impossible task of categorization; impossible both mentally and morally. The variety of human animals is such that any serious effort is foredoomed. But, nonetheless, observation does reveal certain patterns so let us examine them, remembering Jerome Bruner's quote of Neils Bohr: "But there are some things so important that one can only joke about them."

## A GUIDE TO THE WILD LIFE OF ACADEMIA

A full description of Academia would take such a voyager as Captain Cook and a chronicler the like of Mr. Boswell. Being somewhat less than either of these two stalwarts, we shall concern ourselves here with a description of some of the birds that strut, sail, fly, squawk, lay eggs, and otherwise disport themselves in the flora and fauna of this happy land.

COMMON BIRDS IN ACADEMIA IN NO SPECIAL ORDER

*The Horny-Beaked Teacher Trapper.* This one has as its sole *raison d'être* trying to make a fool of the teacher. As this is not a particularly difficult task, he bends to it with a right good will. Adroit handling will make him a good student if you have the patience and fortitude.

*The Red-Throated Croaker.* This bird protests everything with a big squawk. Some built-in Pavlovian reflex makes the first response always a complaint. It is best to wait until the second response, at least.

*The Distant Drum-Marcher.* He marches to a distant drum. Can be distinguished by a far-away glaze over his eyes and an infinite capacity for irrelevancy. Perhaps you can march to his drum, but despair of his marching to yours.

*The Gooney-Jokester.* This forlorn creature gets his sense of identity by being the butt of all the raw humor that characterizes much of this habitat. Resist the temptation to laugh at him; it is doubtful if you can laugh with him.

*The Golden-Halo Worshiper.* This rather pudgy type is characterized by a completely guileless attitude that says, "I am but clay—mold me." "Anything you do must be right because you are you." It is best to hide the feet of clay when confronted by this one.

*The Narrow-Eyed Sharpster.* "Will it be on the test?" "What is the payoff"? are the songs of this bird. Though you may find the thought distressing, he will probably be measured and called a success.

*The Silver-Throated Warbler.* This bird is infatuated with the sound of his own words and is not particularly concerned whether or not they convey any thoughts. In fact, is completely deflated when this is pointed out. Dangerous when cornered because his tongue can be a cutting instrument. More precious than valuable.

*Uniformicus typicus.* Molds happily with the environment and when isolated therefrom asks immediately, "What do you want me to do?" Don't trust him alone—he'll be lost, and often you wish he would get lost.

*Panglossia indeterminata.* This wide-eyed wonderer is completely convinced that this is the best of all possible worlds. Don't stand beneath him; when he falls, it will be with a crash.

*The Faded-Feather Molting Nest-Searcher.* A basic insecurity keeps him close to the nest. He needs constant reassurance that he can step beyond the nest. Rewarding to work with if you have the time and feel like being a Pygmalion. Warning: don't cast a shadow on him—he'll run for cover.

*The Bristle-Beaked Know-It-All.* Has a marked defiance of the instructional process. Fun to tear apart limb by limb and tromp on his feathers. Must resist the temptation because that is often what made him what he is today.

*The Brilliant-Hued Presence.* Really too beautiful to touch and therefore to teach. If you don't believe it just ask her (often a female). Perhaps the best thing to do is to enjoy the view as she will probably be a success anyhow (in her own lights, that is).

*The Grey-Thatched Nest Builder.* Just give him the facts to memorize. And don't give him anything that challenges the pattern of his nest or he will be completely confused. Often when shown a better nest he becomes a rare and wonderful bird.

*The Shifty-Footed Wind Watcher.* A built-in antenna is the hallmark of this bird. Sits back on his position warily until he finds out what the popular position is, then he'll shift to that. Fun to manipulate. Goes into a mad and frantic dance trying to find the new position.

*The Wide-Winged Eagle.* A soaring mind that takes off from your furthest reach. Genuinely creative. Inspiring to work with. Beware because he will often leave you breathless.

*The Happy-Hearted World Watcher.* Serene, confident, self-possessed with a mental pattern marked by a high degree of discrimination. Takes a calm and uncluttered view of the world. No identity crisis. Makes the transition from innocence to wisdom with aplomb. Either marry this one or worship (her or him, depending on your predilection) but resist the temptation of placing him/her in a cage or on a pedestal.

### COMMON ANIMALS OF ACADEMIA LISTED WITH PERTINENT CHARACTERISTICS

*Sharp-Nosed Gos-Sip.* With nose to the ground, ear to the wind, and a foot in every camp, this creature is interested in everything and everybody.

Reaches heights of ecstasy when this interest is proved by telling everything to everybody. Cry: "Who's-with-who, n-o-o-w?"

*El Magnifico.* Everybody, especially students, is supposed to quail in the presence, and those who don't suffer. Apparently doing the world a favor. Cry: "I, I, I," repeated very often.

*Andre Preneur.* Named after an early French explorer. Highly enterprising creature; first to the book room, first with the films, first to the pay office. Cry: "As long as you're up, get me a grant."

*Hollow-Stemmed Standard Bearer.* The subject must be served even at the expense of the students, which it often is. Room has a niche replete with symbols (grades) and offerings (papers) to the great god, standards. Cry: "Come lie on my Procrustean bed, my pretty."

*Roving-Eyed Greek God(dess).* Like the ancient gods, descends from the heights to dally with mere mortals. Not only do the eyes rove but often the hands and feet. Plays with fire but runs like mad. Cry: "Hanky-panky, hanky-panky," often repeated.

*Heavy-Handed Laughing Boy.* Prenatally influenced by old wives' tale: Laugh and world laughs with you. Has been trying ever since and still cries alone. Jokes land with a thud and flop around on the floor. Can't find line between gaiety and vulgarity. Cry: "Have you heard . . ."

*Vicarious Life Fulfiller.* Lives on fringes of other lives, particularly students. Fulfills own life by listening about others. Masks this from self under the guise of interest. Cry: "Come in and tell me about . . ."

*Drooly-Jowled Peeping Tom.* The vicarious life-fulfiller gone sour. All life is seen through a keyhole. When teaching English, leans to the modern paperback; when teaching history is luridly biographical. Cry: "The things kids do these days."

*Square-Backed Stake Seeker.* The academic Joan of Arc martyred on a cross of children. Carries suffering vocally and visibly. Students get the idea that, somehow or other, it is their fault that teacher suffers. Cry: "Many a flower is born to blush unseen and waste its fragrance on the desert air."

*Weary-Shouldered Message Bearer.* Subspecies of above. Differs from above by being resigned rather than martyred. Cry: "Oh, they wouldn't get it, anyhow."

*Gallus-Snapping Harumpher.* Vocally certain that the world is falling apart and the fall will be complete when the new generation takes over. Cry: "Humph, what is the world coming to?"

*Seven-Clawed Child Hater.* Openly and straightforwardly shows distaste for the students. Feeling is cordially reciprocated. Cry: "You can't trust them."

*Two-Footed Spineless Chameleon.* Almost impossible to discern. Blends perfectly with the woodwork. Gives little, demands little. Cry: "I don't rock the boat."

*Vacant-Eyed Pack Runner.* Own decisions are made only after ascertaining how the leader is going. Easily confused with the lemming. Cry: "Good leaders need good followers."

*Empty-Headed Clacker.* Simply the vocal mechanism between the student and the subject. Prattles the book and the authority. Cry: "Klee-shay, klee-shay," often repeated.

*Star-Studded Role Player.* Makes you want to shout, "Will the real you please stand up?" Generally three roles: in class, in faculty meetings, in the smoker. Confuses others, never himself. Cry: "Hi-po-crit, hi-po-crit."

*Quivery-Legged Institution Lover.* All of life wrapped up in institution; therefore contributes little vitality to it. Somehow thinks that institutions are more than the people who are in them. Cry: "I do what is expected of me."

*Heavy-Plated Coracaõ de Ouro.* Beneath a scarred skin beats a heart of gold. Has lived enough to be bitter but somehow has become compassionate. Infinite capacity to listen and to understand. Little amazes, much amuses. Either worshipped or scorned. Cry: Strangled croak midst tears and laughter.

*Long-Viewed Horizon Stretcher.* After almost every contact, learner has a larger view of himself and the world. Each is goaded, challenged, and helped to walk the long path to his own horizons. Cry: "I dare you to be better."

**Helpful Hints for Happy Bird-and-Animal Watching.** One notable characteristic of all of this wild life is that there is a great blending of these characteristics. All birds make all of the noises at one time or another; all the animals have been heard to utter all of these cries at one time or another. But the fact remains that each of them will concentrate his actions in such a way that they fit one of these categories far more often than any other.

These aren't all. One of the joys of the sport is finding new ones. All new ones may be verified by sending them to SCHOOL (The Society for the Collection of Happy Oddballs in Our Land).

## SUMMARY

The phenomena described in this chapter are just that: phenomena. They are rather random and more sensed by the teacher than gained through intellectual insight. But experience and observation will show that they do exist and that minds do change the ideas that they are working with.

There remains one other factor to consider here. Time enters into the system of instruction as one of the dimensions that must be considered. So let us turn to this timely topic.

# chapter ELEVEN

# The Time Factor in Teaching

*. . . a time to every purpose under Heaven.*—Ecclesiastes.

Says the Preacher, "to everything there is a season." Although he didn't become as specific about teaching as he did about many other human endeavors, a shrewd observer can see that time has its effect on the system of instruction as well. If time forces its dimension on the human in the panting struggles that mark his life, it certainly works its inexorable way in the patterns of instruction. Time is a dimension of existence; it is a constraint; it is a shaping force; it is a commodity to be spent; it puts its stamp upon human events. Time is the entity that gives dimension to the melody line; it allows the logic line to have the characteristic of length.

Time is this and it is also an entity to be controlled; it provides a means; it is a channel; it is something to be spent judiciously as a medium of exchange for other time.

So man in his toil and travail times and is timed.

## THE DESCRIPTION OF THE VARIATION

In a real sense these two sides flow into one in the teaching process when we consider the purpose of time in the pattern of instruction. Time is the flow of information that forms the logic line and time controls the amount of the information in the flow across the communications channel. This information becomes the knowledge that in turn becomes the structure in the learner's mind. So that this structure can be formed, the information must come in ordered parts. It is logic that gives the pattern; it is time that gives the amount. This thesis has been pinned on the door in other chapters and is reiterated here so that the effect of time can be added.

**The Obvious Dimensions of Time on the System.** Time works its wonders no less on the student in class than on any other of the human beasts

153

in other conditions of being. Little experience is needed to show the obvious ways in which it makes itself felt.

Any teacher who has watched his class members close their books and begin a suggestive shuffling of feet a few minutes before the end of class understands the influence of time. Little needs to be said for or about administrative fracturing of students' time into class periods. Within this period, the time has its effects. A teacher sensitive to the rhythms of the class can detect high and low points of attentiveness. Sometimes this has a reinforcing circular action; the students are not attentive toward the end so the teacher slacks off, so the students have more reason to be inattentive so the teacher slacks off some more.

Another obvious effect of time is the time of day. It is a smoking-room truism among teachers that the first period in the morning is difficult because the students are sleepy, the periods before lunch are difficult because the students are hungry, the periods after lunch are difficult because the students are sleepy, and the periods before dismissal are difficult because the students are edgy. Which doesn't seem to leave much time that is not difficult.

Any teacher who has faced a class immediately after a pep rally where the students have been urged to make as much noise as possible also sees another effect of the time of day on the students.

The time of the week and the time of the school year have their effects as well. Mondays and Fridays have their traditions—Blue Monday and TGIF are legendary in the school society. There are some intuitive types behind the desk who insist that they can predict a change in the weather by the actions of their class. For many teachers January through March becomes the tunnel to be fought through somehow or other. Fall is all right because the students are happy (relatively) to be free of freedom and Spring is acceptable because the students and the teachers are looking forward to being free of school.

This is all very light and free wheeling and not too susceptible to proof by a scientific procedure. Perhaps some day we will come to grips with the problem, see it for what it is and get in step with the natural rhythms of the seasons of teaching.

**Subtle Dimensions of Time in the System.** Instructors can find a certain rhythm pattern and work within it. In order that this pattern may be examined and described, an assumption must be made. Investigators of teacher behavior have been able to show that the instructional process is rather epidosic in nature. Rather than proceeding in a smooth, never varying flow, instruction seems to proceed in bursts.

Accepting this thesis, examination of these episodes shows a common time allocation into phases. The time point within the episode determines a certain verbal behavior on the part of the instructor or the learner. These episodes are of a short time duration, 5–15 minutes. Thus in the typical class period there seems to be time for about four of these episodes. These four form the structure for the day's learning. Each day's structure in turn becomes a part of a larger whole, the unit.

**The Instructional Episode Analyzed.** Within each of the episodes are four rather distinct time phases: the entry, development, closure, and exit. Each of the episodes within the period can also have these characteristics: the first episode would be the entry, the next developmental, and so on.[1]

The *entry* into the structure of the search image has several purposes. It establishes the contact between learner and instructor and search image. This contact is of a cognitive nature forming the framework within which the necessary cognitive insights can take place. It also fixes certain ground rules for the dialog; what mode it will follow, what logic line is to be pursued, whether the major purpose is product or process. Finally, the entry phase of the episode defines the articulation with preceding search images, with larger ones of which this one is a part. To do this it is necessary in the entry to give the total boundaries or parameters of the search image under examination.

The *development* breaks the whole into its component parts, examines each, and then proceeds to restructure them into a whole once again. To the degree that this restructuring takes place in the learner's mind, instruction takes place. Logic is paramount in this process; the inherent structure of the knowledge determines the order of the presentation of the parts for examination by the dialog.

The *closure* takes place when all the parts are back in place. A necessary ingredient here for the best learning is the discovery by the learner. This phase is made dramatic by the learner experiencing the "aha" phenomenon.

The *exit* provides the bridge to the next search image. It shows the learner how to make the intellectual leap that will enable him to build the structure between search images.

## SOME DIALOGS AND THE CHARTING THEREOF

These then are the four time phases that can be found in a teaching episode. An examination of the four sample dialogs that we have considered can provide examples of these phases.

### THE FIRST DIALOG

ENTRY

I₁. John Marshall's court issued many decisions of far-reaching importance. One of the first and most important was *Marbury* v. *Madison*. So that

---

[1] The idea of the phases for the episode was suggested by some of the work of Dwight Allen and Robert Bush at Stanford University, by B. Othanel Smith in his *Study of the Logic of Teaching* (U.S. Office of Education Cooperative Research Project 258), and by the author's own observations.

we can understand the historical importance of the Marshall court, let's examine this case. Can anyone tell us the details of the case?

L₁. Well, Marbury received an appointment to become a government official and before the commission was signed by Jefferson he went out of office. So Marbury sued Madison, the next president, for it and the court said he could.

DEVELOPMENT

I₂. That's fine—you covered it well but let's look into it a bit further. What was the court order called that Marbury wanted?

L₂. A writ of mandamus?

I₃. That's right. Now what is that?

L₃. An order from a judge to produce a criminal's body.

I₄. No. I think you're talking about a writ of habeas corpus. What is a writ of mandamus?

L₄. (After some hesitation.) That's when a judge orders a court to enforce its own decision.

I₅. Right, but why is that necessary? Isn't a court decision always carried out?

L₅. No.

I₆. Can you give an example?

L₆. The Supreme Court said there should not be segregation in the schools, but there is.

I₇. That's right. (The teacher seems to have missed the point of "all deliberate speed.") But back to the writ. Is there anything more?

L₇. Aha, yes. A court can be forced to issue an order to enforce a law.

CLOSURE

I₈. By Jove, I do believe you've got it. Now, what principle of American government does this illustrate?

L₈. The federal-state relationship?

I₉. Oh no, how could it? What about the *courts*?

L₉. Oh, I know. The separation of powers between the legislators, the executive, and the courts?

I₁₀. No. Doesn't anyone see? The writ of mandamus shows the principle of a government of laws, not men. It means that laws govern men and that the court, being men, can be held accountable to law. That's the importance of a writ of mandamus and that's what *Marbury* v. *Madison* is all about.

EXIT

Now, let's look at another of the decisions of Chief Justice. . . .

**Entry.** In this search image of judicial review, the entry into the structure provides a frame of reference of *Marbury* v. *Madison*. The broader search image of which this is a part is given in the first sentence—John Marshall's court and its importance.

Very little of set is established. The rapport seems to be the rather artificial one of pupils reciting a lesson, standing oral examination on something read. The implication is that it is a task to be done and then forgotten. They have been measured, found not particularly wanting, and are ready for the next.

**Development.** Any discussion of the development is colored by the instructor's rather straightforward attempt to be wrong. His first statement and question in this phase $(I_2)$ puts him on the wrong line and succeeding questions seems to prove that he is bent on pursuing it. A charitable evaluation would be that he is unprepared; a more realistic one is that he is unknowing and compounds the difficulty by being an Empty-Headed Clacker.

**Closure.** This dialog is a good illustration of a traditional type of closure wherein the instructor tells the learner what to know. Unfortunately, of course, it was on the "wrong," or at least an inappropriate, subject. But it has all the proper characteristics: the structure is redefined, the parts are brought into a whole, the significance of the total is shown.

However, this lacks the main ingredient of the closure phase—the sense of discovery by the learner. This recitation of litany ends with the learners being given what to learn and, if there is a sense of discovery, it is a discovery of what teacher wants. Discovery favors the prepared mind; there is no preparation here.

**Exit.** This is not so much an exit as a flight. It is little more than Little Eliza jumping to another ice floe. So the learners ready themselves for yet another recitation.

Probably some learning took place in this episode. Luckily, it was probably very little because it certainly was of the wrong thing.

## Second Dialog

ENTRY

$I_1$. Now, class, for our understanding of underdeveloped nations and why they are that way, let us look at the *sertão* of Brazil. Here on the map up here is the area—it is in the northeast of the country along about here (*indicating its general area with a sweep of the hand*). Now you're all tenth graders and can presumably read a map. From the map, Willie, can you tell me something about this area?

DEVELOPMENT

$L_1$. It's pretty big.

$I_2$. That's right, it is rather extensive. Anything else?

$L_2$. It seems to be a high plain.

$I_3$. High?

L$_3$. Well, higher than the coastline.

I$_4$. That's right, but let's look at another part of the geography. What about this small rainfall map here—what does that say to us?

L$_4$. There isn't any.

I$_5$. Any?

L$_5$. Well, very little.

I$_6$. That's right—it's a desert almost. But can it be a desert with this river running here (*pointing to the Rio São Francisco*)?

L$_6$. Sure, because it isn't a real desert. There just isn't enough regular rain.

I$_7$. That's right, it's desert like the American southwest rather than the Sahara. But let's turn to another side of the picture—the economic. Your text doesn't say much about this so let me make a few points about it. The major thing to understand is that it is a land of poverty. The annual income is less than $30 per year. This is a grinding poverty that means there is little to buy or sell and that there is a direct consumption of food produced. The soil is poor; the farming methods are primitive so there is only a bare minimum produced. Much of the land is owned by someone from the cities, and these absentee landlords are not interested in improving things too much, generally speaking.

The people are poor and they have few schools. The illiteracy rate is very high and so is the birth rate. They are superstitious and have a mystique about their land. During the many dry years there will be quite a migration out of the *sertão* to the big cities of the south and coast. Then when the rains return (as they must by the law of averages) the word seems to get around and the people begin to return to the *sertão*. Even though it is a completely marginal land, they have the feeling that it will be good someday. So they keep on. This is a land of legends. The men are often *vaqueiros* riding after scrawny cattle through the *caatinga*, a scrubby plant with a spiny growth much like our mesquite in the west.

L$_7$. This seems to be like the west in our country with cowboys and everything. Don't you suppose that it will naturally change into something good as our west did?

I$_8$. That is an analogy that is made often, but I don't think that it is a good one. For one thing, the American west didn't have much population, and this does—about 40,000,000. To make the analogy correct, you would have to have 40,000,000 people in Utah, Arizona, Nevada, and New Mexico. So, Mr. Teacher-trapper, you didn't trap me after all.

CLOSURE

But what does this all add up to?

L$_8$. I guess that this part of Brazil is underdeveloped because it doesn't have much rain and the people are poor and illiterate.

I$_9$. That's right as far as it goes, but let's not get trapped into thinking that there is a connection between rain and development. The connection is between geographic base and development, and rainfall is only a part of that base.

EXIT

Now what are some other factors that cause underdevelopment? Are there any questions?

**Entry.** This entry is routine. It doesn't establish any rapport in a set; if it does the rapport is that that comes from a situation based on extrinsic motivation of force and sugar-coated by some friendly phrases. The tie-in to any previous, or larger, search image is quick and probably unnoticed. The description of the whole search image is accomplished by a wave of the hand at the map.

**Development.** This phase is based on the learning task of getting information from a map and the learner goes through the needed intellectual process of reading a map. At the point I$_7$ the instructor makes a necessary shift in information source. The map doesn't contain enough, the book doesn't contain enough, so, in an expository fashion, the instructor becomes the information source for other parts of the search image.

**Closure.** This is the right thing done in the right way with minimal results. The learners (at least one of them) made a discovery. But it wasn't quite a discovery of the whole structure. The instructor was content at this point to let the closure enclose only a part—the geographic base, particularly rainfall. He had a sense of error here because he did warn the learners of the intellectual trap. The succeeding search image then became a part of this one.

**Exit.** So a basic intellectual confusion is perpetrated here. The search image is the example of the *sertão* as an underdeveloped area. The various parts of the concept of "underdevelopment" are developed and when the closure closed on but one, the instructor goes back to other parts *as if they were of a new search image.* He should have done it as a correction of a closure rather than leave the impression that he was going to something new.

A final word about this exit: one of the dreariest clichés in teaching is the final, "Are there any questions?" In reality, this question is a mere formality. Both learner and instructor would be surprised if anyone violated unwritten codes by asking a question. Often the real meaning is, "Well, we've beat that horse to death; now, if there are no interruptions, let's find another."

## THIRD DIALOG

ENTRY

I$_1$. In our continuing discussion of civil rights and responsibilities let's look at another one. I have here a clipping that says that a government official is proposing that all of the information about each person in the U.S. that is contained in various agencies be brought together and stored in a giant computer where it could be recalled at any time. What do you think about this?

DEVELOPMENT

$L_1$. It seems to be a good idea.

$I_2$. Why?

$L_2$. Well, all of the stuff needed would be in one spot.

$I_3$. Why is this information needed?

$L_{3(1)}$. So that the people that need to know can know what they need to know.

$L_{3(2)}$. Yeah, but why do they need to know?

$L_{3(3)}$. Maybe I don't want them to know something about me!

$L_{3(4)}$. (General murmurings of chidings of ill will about what he has done that should be secret.)

$I_4$. Let's look at this a moment. We're just airing opinions now; perhaps we can do more. Let's put them together into an examination of something. What is the problem posed by this use of the computer?

$L_4$. Everybody will know everybody's secrets.

$I_5$. Perhaps that is an overgeneralization; perhaps it could be phrased a little better. What civil right seems to be endangered?

$L_5$. Freedom of speech?

$I_6$. No.

$L_6$. Freedom of assembly?

$I_7$. No, and I think that you are guessing. One of the Congressmen said that this is an invasion of personal privacy. Willie?

$L_{7(1)}$. I read about that in some magazines where they were talking about all the bugs in rooms.

$L_{7(2)}$. Oh yeah, where the olive in the martini is a radio that sends a message.

$L_{7(3)}$. I seen a movie where a girl had a microphone in her—

$I_8$. (Interrupting hastily for he, too, had seen the film and where the microphone was hidden.) There has been a lot of discussion about the use of these electronic devices. But— Yes, Willie?

$L_8$. Can the police tap the telephones?

$I_9$. Do you mean "can" or "may"?

$L_9$. It doesn't make much difference. Can they?

$I_{10}$. It does make a difference. It is possible to do it but whether they have the permission to do it or not is another question.

$L_{10}$. Well, do they?

$I_{11}$. They do, but they are not always supposed to. Now what about the hypothesis: is this an invasion of the right of privacy?

$L_{11}$. How do these computers work?

$I_{12}$. Don't be impertinent, young man. Answer the question.

$L_{12}$. Yes, teacher, it is an invasion of the right of privacy.

CLOSURE

$I_{13}$. You're right. It has been called that. Can you tell me why you answered it that way?

$L_{13}$. *(In a voice audible only to his classmates.)* Because that's the answer you wanted.

$I_{14}$. *(With professional cheeriness.)* The bell will ring soon, so that's all for today. Tomorrow we will discuss one of our most valuable freedoms—freedom of speech.

**Entry.** This entry differs from the others in that it immediately asks that the mode of operation be considered as hypothetical. There is no articulation with the search image which preceded, and the overview is rather sketchy.

**Development.** The major characteristics about this development is that it never comes full circle; it continues in a linear fashion and, instead of coming to a logical conclusion, it peters out like a freshet stream in the desert. The learners contributed to this, of course, with their rather cynical questions, such as $L_{11}$.

**Closure.** Consequently, what closure there is is caused by the learner who seems to know how to follow the system. He did what he was told.

**Exit.** Again, a flight rather than an exit.

## Fourth Dialog

ENTRY

$I_1$. Class, here on the board is a sentence. (Kennedy could not have been elected in 1960 if Stevenson hadn't been elected in 1952 and 1956.) As you can see it is not absolutely provable—no one can say that it is completely true or false. But it is well worth looking at. We are not so much interested in facts to be memorized as we are in bringing the facts together into a logical thought process. So let us speculate about this. What does this statement compare?

DEVELOPMENT

$L_1$. It doesn't compare anything.

$I_2$. I mean, what does it ask you to compare as you think about it.

$L_2$. Kennedy and Stevenson?

$I_3$. That's right. But before we compare them what else 's in that statement on the board? It has to do with the comparison of time.

$L_3$. I guess the elections of 1952, '56, and '60.

$I_4$. That's right—you people deserve the reputation of being a good group. Now come the key questions. Should we look for likenesses or differences between Stevenson and Kennedy?

L$_4$. Likenesses.

I$_5$. That's right; you're very good. Why did you say that?

L$_5$. (*Sheepishly.*) I just guessed.

I$_6$. (*Lamely, amidst laughter.*) Well, it was a good guess. (*Recovering.*) It was a good guess but right because, according to the postulate, Kennedy built on Stevenson. Or another way of saying it, Stevenson paved the way. So voters looked for similar things. So what were these likenesses?

L$_6$. Excuse me for saying this, but I hardly remember Kennedy and I don't remember Stevenson at all. All I can remember of the 1956 election is that we voted in the third grade and Eisenhower won.

I$_7$. Oh, I guess I had forgotten how young the young are—or how old I am. What does the book say?

L$_{7(1)}$. Very little about Stevenson except that he was governor of Illinois.

L$_{7(2)}$. And that nobody could have won against Eisenhower.

L$_{7(3)}$. It doesn't say that; it just says that Eisenhower was a very popular war hero and that after every war but one we had elected one.

L$_{7(2)}$. Well, I was just practicing what the teacher calls "inference."

I$_8$. That's what he was doing. I guess the book doesn't help us here so let me add what I can. It seems to me that where Stevenson and Kennedy were alike was in their feeling for the intellect. Both of them were expert in the use of words; their speeches are marvelous reading. In fact, Stevenson spent so much time polishing his speeches that his aides often despaired because he was neglecting other parts of campaigning. This characteristic of his—his intellectual quality—often was used against him. He was called an "egghead." To many people in that time there was something wrong in being interested in the world of ideas, in using graceful words. His defense against this was often a merry quip. One of his comments was "Eggheads of the world unite—you have nothing to lose but your yolks." And another time speaking at Harvard, in March 1964, he said,

> Confronted, surrounded indeed, as I am here in Cambridge tonight by more highly educated fellow citizens than I have ever faced, and inadequately prepared, I am uncomfortably reminded of the abiding truth of those classic words that never occurred to Horace: *"Via ovicipitum dura est,"* or for the benefit of the engineers among you: "The way of the egghead is hard."

L$_8$. He seemed to be quite a wit. Wasn't—didn't Kennedy make a lot jokes, too?

I$_9$. Certainly. Since his death there have been many collections published containing his jokes and quips.

L$_9$. Tell us some of them.

EXIT

$I_{10}$. There goes the bell. I'll save them for tomorrow.

**Entry.** This is a straightforward entry. The dialog established immediately establishes that the accent is more on the process than the product. The learner finds that the "ground rules" have been declared; he is not to recite as much as he is to relate. Also there is no attempt to articulate this with a past search image. These two conditions may turn the dialog from a common search to a general bull session.

**Development.** In a way the dialog turned into the general bull session as the instructor was drawn by the attractions of the subject; the temptation to tell stories to a fresh audience was too much.

The exchange in $I_4$ and $L_4$ is typical. The question with its either/or, fifty-fifty chance tempted guessing more than reasoning.

**Closure.** There really wasn't any formal attempt made by the instructor to have any closure. It is altogether conceivable, however, that one did take place in the learner's mind, and it probably left the impression that the search image was the wit of Stevenson.

**Exit.** This was an end rather than an exit. Here time controlled the instructor; he certainly didn't exercise any timing.

## CONSIDERATIONS GOVERNING THE INSTRUCTOR'S CHOICE

Handling the phases of the teaching episodes offers a wide variety of choices to the instructor as he operates within the system of instruction. Within the constraints of time available and timing mechanisms he has a wide range of choices for action. These are impossible to delineate here. They are unique within each episode. No formulas can be given; all that can be done is to describe the arena within which the instructor will make his decision and give some examples of dialogs within which commentary can be made. However, a general consideration must be described.

**The Necessary Coincidence of the Learning Cycle, the Bit of Knowledge and the Instructional Episode.** Previous sections of this volume have examined some of the other patterns that fit into the system of instruction; the pattern of learning and its time dimensions, the size of the bit of knowledge and its time dimensions. Now it remains for the instructor to bring these into a necessary coincidence. It is rather senseless to be concerned with the instructional episode and the nuances necessary to bring it into fruition if the instructor is trying to teach a bit of knowledge that is too large to fit into the episode. Or if the instructional episode overlaps the attention span of the learner, the necessary attentiveness to the idea is lost and the time is wasted.

So, in some way or another, the instructor must find the resources to bring these three cycles of timing into a congruence so that instruction can take place. Finding this means is the art of teaching; describing the phenomenon is the science of teaching.

## SUGGESTED READING

ALLEN, DWIGHT W., and RICHARD E. GROSS. "Microteaching, A New Beginning for Beginners," *NEA Journal* (December, 1965), pp. 25–26.

# POSTLUDE

# chapter TWELVE

# A Concluding Passage

*The life which is unexamined is not worth living.*—SOCRATES.

So we come to the end of the line; this inquiry into a system for instruction has been an examination of the logic line that forms the structure of the idea for a system for instruction. Along this line we have pointed out the increasing importance of the social enterprise of education and the necessity of developing a systematic study of the formal, ordered instructional process with a model for the system. Given the need for such a system, then components of it must be examined. So within the structure of a system for instruction are three primary component parts: the subject to be learned, the learner's mind, and the instructor's mind. The examination then proceeded to these three components of the logic line with a final closure around the structure coming in a model for the system of instruction.

Now the analogy of the melody line becomes useful. Musical compositions attain a grandeur from the subtleties of variation on the melody line. Melody often has a shimmering brilliance of its own; to adorn that melody with the variations is to bring out its much more enduring and deeper brilliance. Melody is the rather miraculous product of a spontaneous intuition. But the innocent melody is not enough; complete composition results from artistic shaping by gentle, caring hands dedicated to bringing from the melody depths and heights only dreamt of.

And so it is in the system of learning. The logic line is embellished by an artistry with an analytic base until all the nuances are polished. The next parts of the system that were examined were some of the components that act as variations on this logic line to bring out all of its qualities. The ordering of the knowledge, the strategies for instruction, the actions of minds on the ideas, the sense of time on the ideas are all variations that act on the theme.

So we come to the end of the logic line; now that the structure has been described and analyzed there remains a haunting question. It is the rather pragmatic question that concerns proof: "It all sounds acceptable, but how can I be sure that I am performing in that system?" So some models have been pointed out that can act as mechanisms for self-evaluation.

These dialogs and comments are not intended to serve as anything but examples of analysis. It would be a folly of the boldest sort to suggest that the "good" can be defined in a book far removed from the array of particular circumstances that make up a class. A system of instruction can be defined and described and models given within it. But as a melody awaits the musician's hand, this system awaits the instructor's artistry.

A final word for the instructor as he takes his place in the educational enterprise. His students start the journey to the thresholds of their own minds in his classroom. Over the portals of that room, to be seen by the students who enter, should be inscribed Hamlet's words: "There are more things in heaven and earth, Horatio, than are dreamt of in your philosophy." With this as a guide, perhaps they will look to the far horizons of learning and reach for the new products of that knowledge.

And as they leave that class to continue the journey, untutored and unafraid, it would be fitting that the last words they saw, carved over the door of the classroom, urged them to continue with the task of learning. One of the strivings that is the power and the glory of the human condition is the drive of curiosity, the need to light candles in dark corners, the refusal to curse the darkness. All of this Socrates said so well: ". . . the life that is unexamined is not worth living."

Now all that remains is to sit under a tree and watch the human procession as it journeys from its earth to its heaven, as it examines its life and dreams of its philosophies. It is to be hoped that the ludicrous scramble may perhaps be tempered into a sense of ordered purpose by a haunting melody which plays over God's children and casts its glow upon them as they struggle from travail to serenity, from ludicrocity[1] to grace, from loneliness to solitude, from scorn to concern, from innocence to wisdom.

---

[1] How laughingly absurd
   is the very word
   Ludicrousness
How delightfully firm
   is the invented term
   Ludicrocity

# Index